I0213140

THE ARKANSAS HITCHHIKE KILLER

JAMES WAYBERN "RED" HALL

JANIE NESBITT JONES

THE
History
PRESS

Published by The History Press
Charleston, SC
www.historypress.com

Copyright © 2021 by Janie Nesbitt Jones
All rights reserved

First published 2021

ISBN 9781540246370

Library of Congress Control Number: 2020948551

Notice: The information in this book is true and complete to the best of our knowledge. It is offered without guarantee on the part of the author or The History Press. The author and The History Press disclaim all liability in connection with the use of this book.

All rights reserved. No part of this book may be reproduced or transmitted in any form whatsoever without prior written permission from the publisher except in the case of brief quotations embodied in critical articles and reviews.

This book is dedicated to my father, Gordon Nesbitt, the dream-weaver, and to my husband, Wyatt Jones, who made my dreams come true.

CONTENTS

AUTHOR'S NOTE

This book is about the life and crimes of serial killer James Waybern "Red" Hall. It is based on newspaper and magazine articles, court documents, and interviews with people who interacted with Hall personally. Though many of the conversations and events in the narrative are my dramatic interpretations of what was said and done, I have tried to be as faithful to the truth as possible. I have quoted much of the dialogue verbatim from accounts by the primary reporter on the case and from testimonies of witnesses as recorded in the trial transcript. Recollections of those who knew him were invaluable to me as I tried to acquire a sense of who this man was and why he committed such dreadful deeds. Some names have been changed by request.

Acknowledgements

For their contributions in making this book possible, I offer my sincerest gratitude to the following people:

Jim Chandler, historian of the 455th Anti-Aircraft Artillery Battalion (World War II); Kevin Ellis, managing editor of the *Gaston Gazette*; Bill Cook, cousin of Corporal Charles W. Nipper III; the staff at the Faulkner County Library; Alicia Jones with UCA's Torreyson Library; Melinda Herder, director of the Humboldt Public Library; Claudia Beck with the Seminole Public Library; Adele Heagney with the St. Louis Public Library; and Kathryn Fitzhugh from the UALR William H. Bowen School of Law.

I also want to thank Vicki Vowell, founder of *AY Magazine*, who helped me find my calling in true crime; Rhonda Love for her wise counseling and for believing in me when I didn't believe in myself; Dr. Jeffrey Marotte, who played a vital role in the completion of this narrative by saving my life, literally; Dr. Tyrone Lee, who saved my life a second time; Chad Rhoad, senior acquisitions editor at Arcadia Publishing, for his patience and guidance; The History Press production editor Abigail Fleming, with her keen eye for detail; and all the staff at Arcadia Publishing for their roles in producing the book.

I thank all my friends and family members for exhibiting saintly patience and good humor while I talked obsessively about the subject of this chronicle. In conclusion, I couldn't have fulfilled my desire to finish the story of Red Hall without my dear and talented husband, Wyatt Jones, who always has my back.

1

EL DIABLO

There is a community in Faulkner County, Arkansas, called Happy Valley, where springtime comes dressed in yellow flowers, and summer's stifling heat is tempered by the ice creamy smoothness of July's blue skies. In autumn, the wooded hills around the vale adorn Mother Nature's breast with garnet, coral and amber brooches. Winter covers everything with a swansdown blanket. This seemingly idyllic setting is a seductive sham, for it once produced a man whose heart was as dark as night.

Happy Valley lies between Hardin Hill and Whitmore Mountain to the south and east and Bailey and White Oak Mountains to the west and north, respectively. Actually, "mountain" is a misnomer, because the highest peak, White Oak, at only 639 feet, falls far short of the 2,000-foot height requirement to qualify as a mountain, but it passes as such in a state where the highest point of land is Mount Magazine (2,753 feet), located near the little town of Paris in Logan County.

At the time this story took place, Happy Valley comprised a few farms loosely connected to nearby neighborhoods that included McGintytown, Marcus Hill and Barney. The social hub was the town of Enola, where the post office was located. Pioneers who settled in the area found the land to be fertile and productive, and it still seems to be an uncommonly favorable environment for health and longevity. It could be wagered that more nonagenarians reside in Enola and surrounding communities than anywhere else in Arkansas. Many residents have lived to see the century mark and beyond.

Happy Valley, where it all began. *Photo by Wyatt Jones.*

Among the early arrivals in Happy Valley were the Hall and Ingram families. The Ingrams bought farmland in 1859 and built a dogtrot log house about one hundred feet from the old Little Rock–Clinton Road. In the dogtrot style of architecture, two cabins were connected by a roofed passageway where saddles, tack, farm implements and household articles hung from pegs on the walls, but the primary purpose of the breezeway was to provide more comfortable sleeping arrangements during the hot, humid summers.

The Hall family moved to the area in 1906 and built their home also just off the old Little Rock–Clinton Road near the Ingrams. The house had a wraparound porch, and the yard was immaculately kept. Daffodils, narcissus and irises bordered the walkway that led from the front gate to the house. To the left of the gate was a flowering quince tree, and to the right was a large persimmon tree that bore fragrant white blossoms in late spring and sweet fruit in the fall. Raccoons had a field day with the delicacy.

Two members of the Hall and Ingram families became more than neighbors on September 14, 1913, when Eva Lorena Ingram married Samuel Jerome Hall. They had ten offspring, five boys and five girls. Another child died in infancy. Samuel was a farmer and a preacher in the Primitive Baptist Church. Religion was an important function for the family and their kin. A lot of baptisms took place in Cadron Creek about a mile south of Happy Valley. Sometimes on Sundays after a worship service of preaching, prayers and a cappella singing, young people would gather at the Cadron Bridge and socialize.

Eva and Samuel's fourth-born was James Waybern, though he was better known by his nickname, Red. He had wavy red hair that was the envy of many a little girl. One day when he was visiting his cousins, he led them and his three older siblings into the woods and found a sizable tree stump, which he turned into a pulpit. Imitating his father's oratorical style, he proceeded to give a spirited sermon. "He was really going good," a cousin said, "Until one in the group stepped on a hornets' nest." The sermon stopped abruptly after the little girl was stung on her arms and neck and had to be carried up to the house where Red's grandmother eased the painful stings with a poultice made of dipping snuff, right out of the dipper's mouth, an effective remedy for wasp, bee and hornet stings. The abbreviated biblical lecture was the last time Red commanded a congregation, for in a few years, people who knew him would say he was never what you would call "sitting in the front pew of the church."

Red and his cousins enjoyed spending time at their grandparents' place because they had plenty of space to play in the yard. On clear winter days, they could roll around on the dead Bermuda grass on the south lawn, protected from the north wind by the house with its fireplace against the south wall. If they needed a nap, a comfy bed in the living room was always available.

Grandmother Hall was an excellent cook, known especially for her apple pies, dill pickles and chicken and dressing. She grew her own sage for the dressing and, of course, raised chickens. When the occasion arose for such a meal, she was in charge, starting with the killing of the main course. Catching one of the fowl that she had fed, fattened and fawned over, she grabbed it by the neck and twisted its body until the cervical vertebra broke. Then she cut the head off and tossed the body to the ground where it performed an awkward dance with death before flopping down and lying still. She drained it by hanging it upside down and afterward boiled it to facilitate the plucking process.

Death, in all forms and species, was a part of life. Hog killing time was a cause for celebration. After the year's first cold spell, neighbors got together and had a high ol' time socializing at the expense of the hog. After slaughtering the animal, they dunked it in a fifty-gallon wash pot filled with scalding water, making it easier to remove the hair. Then they used ropes and pulleys attached to a strong tree limb to hoist the animal by its hooves. One of the men took a knife, split the hog open and eviscerated it. Nothing was thrown away—not even the bladder, which became an inflated balloon for the children to toss back and forth. Red was usually in the midst of all the fun. His daddy was the man who actually killed the hog, shooting it right between the eyes and then slitting its throat.

The children of Happy Valley were accustomed to the day-to-day chore of providing meat for the family. Most did not escalate to the killing of their fellow human beings. But one did, and this is his story.

TO THE OUTSIDE WORLD, Samuel Jerome Hall was a well-respected man of the cloth, devoted to following the Good Book. That he was a stern disciplinarian with his children was just another way he lived by the Word of God. But his pious mien disguised a sadistic, foul-tempered side that only his family saw. His brother, John Phillip Hall, was the exact opposite; he earned the love and respect of his wife and children with his kind and gentle nature. One of John's daughters, Connie, said, "Uncle Sam was meaner than a junkyard dog," and she recalled an incident she witnessed as a child that caused her to look at her uncle as "a preacher with horns. Diablo," she said.

John Hall owned a farm with bottomland, and on one occasion when Sam and his family had come over to help in the fields, Red said something that enraged his father.

"I saw him beat that poor little boy with a cotton stalk, branches and all," Connie recalled. "Beat him something terrible. Like an animal. I'd never seen anyone do that. I guess Red was about ten or twelve years old."

Sam Hall's family was, indeed, a troubled one. His wife, Eva, was a mouse, unable to talk back to her overbearing, demanding husband. Her father and mother were cousins, and some of Eva's siblings had mental problems; one brother seldom had a conversation with anyone but himself, another was considered a moron and a third took off as a hobo; it was discovered later that he had been killed.

Sam and Eva's first child, Lucy, was born in 1914 and was mentally disabled. She went to school until the third grade but couldn't follow instructions and couldn't control her kidneys, no matter how many times the teacher told her it was okay to run to the outhouse without asking for permission. She was sent home as often as three times a day after having an accident that went all over her chair and the floor, a disruption that nauseated some children and caused others to laugh. The teacher and Lucy's parents agreed it would be better for everyone to pull her out of school permanently.

Lucy's siblings, except for Red, were otherwise average, and for that matter, Red was healthy, aside from a bout of typhoid fever when he was around four years old. He grew to be a strapping young fellow and was the only one in the household who would stand up and talk back to his father. It was difficult to say which one had the bigger ego. The father recognized himself in Red, and Red could see himself in his father, and neither one liked what he saw. Though Sam was hard on his entire family, he unleashed his wrath on Red with greater frequency and with more ferocity. Della Fogerty, an acquaintance of Red's, put forth the idea that Preacher Sam saw his son's red hair as a sign of heresy and betrayal. Was not Judas red-haired? Whatever the reason for Sam's intolerance toward his own progeny will never be known, but it should come as no surprise that the little boy slipped away into the woods as often as he could, sometimes traveling around the entire county. But his father chased after him and dragged him back home, an inconvenience that riled the man to no end.

Later, while still just barely a teenager, Red started staying away for longer intervals, wandering even farther astray to other states. At the age of fourteen, he journeyed to Topeka, Kansas, where he cut corn to make a little money. Shortly before that, however, he sustained a head injury. Stories handed down give different versions of what happened. His father said the following:

> We were hauling hay when he was twelve or thirteen, and he was a big boy. He wanted to help. He was dragging hay to the baler with a pole in each hand. We would be on the other side of the haystack pulling with a mule, and he let a pole slip over and strike him on the back of the head. He was unconscious an hour or so. We put him in the truck and took him to Dr. H.H. Hardy's home for treatment.

Another scenario of the "accident" went like this: "Red sustained an injury by one of his fellow workers who dropped a fence rail off a rail stack onto his head, and he was knocked unconscious."

But relatives, who knew the preacher man for what he really was, suspected he had whacked his obstreperous son once too often and a little too hard.

Red was sick and nervous and not himself for several days after the injury, and it was two or three weeks before he recovered completely. Some people said he was never himself again.

"Red was not the easiest person to have a conventional conversation with," Della Fogerty said.

> *He tended to be a little agitated at times, not too focused. He would have times when he was perfectly normal, then he would kind of go off the deep end. He went through different cycles in his mentality. Neighbors said he would walk around at night peeping in windows and do stuff like that, and then there'd be times when he would go into a rage for no obvious reason. It was referred to then as "mentally disturbed." You know how gossip gets around in rural communities, and that was back in the days when we didn't have the technology we have now.*

Gossip, rumors and whispered innuendoes are powerful weapons to use against anyone who is different or unwelcome. In her memoir, *Happy Valley Memories*, Connie Weir wrote about an incident involving a couple whose reception upon moving to the valley went from chilly to chilling when they awoke one morning to find their horse lying in the barnyard with its throat cut. Whether or not the horse's owners knew what transgression had made them the target of such reprehensible behavior, they got the message and moved out of the territory.

One rumor that followed Red around was the unexplained absence of his brother Gilmore George Hall, referred to by his father as "Gilmer." Gilmore was married at least once, in 1934, when he was sixteen years old. He and his fourteen-year-old bride had one child, a daughter. In 1936, he left home without a word. It was said that when he fathered another baby girl, possibly out of wedlock, he saw the infant on the morning she was born and then left, never to return. Later, when Red's compulsions became front page news, a lot of people wondered if he had assumed a role in Gilmore's fate.

Some gossip that Red had heard as a child grew to legendary proportions, and one of those tales made a deep impression on him. It was the story of Jonathan Hardin, who arrived in Faulkner County in 1840 and built a two-story house at the busy intersection of the Lewisburg-Searcy, Des Arc–Springfield and Little Rock–Clinton Roads. Located atop a hill above a drainage ditch connected to the East Fork of the Cadron, Hardin's house also served as an inn and tavern to the many travelers passing through on their way to market with their livestock, produce and other goods. After finishing their business in Little Rock, on their way home, flush with money, they would stop over once more at Hardin Inn. Folks thereabouts heard that some of those guests were never seen again. Meanwhile, Jonathan Hardin grew richer and richer. Ultimately, he owned 5,500 acres, a coal mine, a blacksmith shop, a cotton gin and fifteen slaves. The story goes that Hardin robbed and murdered some of the sojourners, dismembered them and threw their heads into the drainage ditch. This disposal site became known as "the hainted ditch," and many a child and more than a few adults avoided the hainted ditch when at all possible. A man who went looking for his missing brother at Hardin Inn disappeared, and when his father and uncle came along about a month later, they found his emaciated horse, dead from starvation and thirst, still tied to a tree in the woods near the inn.

Red Hall thought the supposedly murdered travelers should have known better. How easy it must have been, he conjectured, to lure the unsuspecting souls with a smile and a drink and then dispatch them from this world of woe and into the afterlife.

In Jonathan Hardin's defense, he was never charged with the gruesome crimes attributed to him by gossipmongers. But the legend was to be his legacy, for the money and possessions he acquired did nothing to prevent what some might say was a curse on his family. He outlived all but one of his sons; two were Civil War casualties, and one died from a wasp sting. The son who survived never married and never had children, meaning no more male heirs to carry on the family name.

Several schools were in proximity to Happy Valley: Union Gap, Cadron Gap, Cadron Valley and Marcus Hill. Most of them consolidated with the Enola school system in the late 1930s, but Red had moved on by then. He'd gone to school regularly enough to be promoted from the eighth grade to the ninth but dropped out in early 1937 when he couldn't refuse the beckoning call of the open road. This was at a time when hobos were a familiar sight along the American backroads. They were mostly honest men who hopped trains in search of employment, and they drew a distinction between themselves and tramps. Hobos worked for their meals. Tramps didn't. The public, however, sometimes used the terms interchangeably, especially in rural households without men. Farm women often needed help with the hard labor in the fields, but when only a screened door separated them from a scruffy-looking stranger, the ladies were suspicious and turned the itinerant away. They gave little thought to the possibility that

James Waybern "Red" Hall.
Illustration by Wyatt Jones.

the hobos themselves might become victims of foul play. In one year alone, 6,500 were killed in the United States. Even after the Depression, men still rode the rails, but the increased use of cars and trucks signaled a decline in travel by train. Rovers such as Red adapted. He found hitching rides to his liking. He seemed to come by it naturally.

When school let out in the summer of '38, two other Faulkner County boys, sixteen-year-old Jackie Anthony and his cousin Johnny, decided to go hitchhiking, too, only they had a particular destination in mind. They had heard about guys going to Detroit and getting good jobs in the auto industry there. The problem was their age; the factories weren't hiring workers that young. The boys didn't want to return to Arkansas, and after a short discussion, they opted to hitchhike to California.

"We got to Okmulgee, Oklahoma," Jackie recalled.

A branch ran under a nice bridge right there in town next to a big grocery store. We got a job there and made forty cents a day apiece. It kept food in our bellies. We slept under that bridge, and you'd be surprised at what a good bed that was. We were helping them clean up at the store one Friday evening, getting ready for the weekend. We worked all day, and they gave us a dollar apiece, so now we're in the money. We were sitting there in the early evening—it was still light—and we had just finished our meal when we saw a guy coming down the street. Now, Red Hall ran—he didn't walk—he ran left-handed. In other words, he travelled sideways, the left part of his body first, and he was running, so the first thing Johnny and I thought was that maybe he had stolen something and the law was after him. He came up to us, recognized us, and said, "Tell me something. Do you boys have any money?" We told him, "No, no." He had nothing else to say and took off, left foot first, the way he went.

The year 1938 was an important one for Red. It was during this time that two momentous events occurred in his life. He met his first wife, and according to him, he committed his first eleven murders.

2

LOVE AND MARRIAGE

Though Red seldom attended religious services, he had seen a young lady at the Marcus Hill Church one Sunday and decided meeting her would be worth the boredom of a sermon, so he spruced himself up and went.

He introduced himself with a broad grin, saying, "I'm James Waybern Hall." Pointing to his hair, he added, "But everybody calls me 'Red.'"

"I'm Walcie McKey," said the pretty brunette. She was of medium build, but standing next to her five-foot-eleven, 170-pound suitor, she seemed more petite.

"I've seen you here before," he said.

"Been comin' here most of my life. Mama and I live there," she pointed to a house next door to the church.

"That's handy," he said.

"Yeah," she nodded.

Neither one was a big talker, but if either dominated the sparse conversation, it was Red. He did a little bragging, and she was enthralled by stories about his trips away from home. Walcie never got to go anywhere, and the most entertainment she ever had was when the church would have all-day singings and dinner on the ground. Transportation in 1938 Arkansas was still limited to people who could afford cars, and not a lot of rural dwellers fell into that category. Living a sheltered and somewhat isolated existence, Walcie had little interaction with the male population and didn't date. She was sometimes taunted by classmates because of her naïveté and modesty. She once asked her friend Della Fogerty, "Why do they tease me like that?"

Della answered, "Well, look at me. They tease me all the time, too, 'cause I'm short and red-headed and freckle-faced. I just don't pay any attention to it."

Della wasn't surprised that Walcie fell for Red. Many years later, she recalled, "When Red came along, he had the right things to say, and it was understandable. They were just two entirely different personalities."

During his courtship of Walcie, Red continued to live his life on a whim, traveling about whenever the urge struck him. He passed through Kansas several times, stopping just long enough either to earn money the honest way or to take money from somebody who needed it just as much as he did.

Red was especially partial to the upland region of the Great Plains in the heart of Kansas. The roadways stretched for miles with only an occasional farmhouse or granary dotting the countryside. Red appreciated the vast solitude because it allowed him to see approaching vehicles at a distance, giving him time to formulate a plan. Would he engage the driver in friendly conversation and then rob the unsuspecting victim, or would he just ride on into the next town? Good fortune was with his benefactor when Red chose the second option.

In 1938, Red took temporary employment on a farm outside of Salina, Kansas. The sign on an arch above the city's Union Pacific Depot read, "Salina: Your Opportunity." Industrious people saw potential for prosperity in the slogan, but Red saw the same old drudgery. After toiling in the fields all day, he liked to take in the sights and sounds of the town at night. It was the place to be on a Saturday past sundown. With the worst dust storms of the Great Depression three years behind them and the threat of war in Europe just a specter in the future, Salinians were doing well.

One source of pride for Salina was Cozy Inn Hamburgers, a popular café still in existence today. Located on North Seventh Street, the Cozy became famous for its hamburgers, also called sliders because the fry cooks would put the burgers on wax paper and slide them down the counter to salivating customers. The sliders were crowned with pickles, ketchup, mustard and a smothering of onions. Red washed his burgers down with a bottle of grape Nehi soda pop.

Aromas from the Cozy Inn wafted clear over to the next block on North Santa Fe Avenue, where people gathered in nightclubs for an evening of music and dance. Ella Fitzgerald's "A-Tisket, A-Tasket," Glenn Miller's

"Doin' the Jive" and Fats Waller's syncopated rhythms put a pep in the step of sidewalk passersby.

While many of the weekend partiers were already paired off, a few were either enjoying their own company or looking for someone else—a friend, a stranger, it didn't matter. But such a chance encounter for one woman was very unfortunate timing. She was intrigued by the color of his hair. He was intrigued by the color of her skin. A bright smile, red lipstick and the swirl of a purple skirt. A dark alley. An impulse. The caprice of Providence. Two people entered the alley, but only one came out.

WALCIE SAW RED REGULARLY for about eight months, and six months after that they got married. The ceremony took place on July 16, 1939, in the Enola home of Mr. and Mrs. E.J. Hoggard, with the groom's father officiating. The newlyweds rented some land at Enola where Walcie's mother, Amanda, moved in with them and helped keep house while Red farmed. The landowner would get part of the crop, and in return, he sold a portion of the land to the Halls. But if Walcie thought they would settle into a comfortable, blissful married life, she had another thought coming. Matrimony didn't calm Red's rambling ways.

One evening in November 1940, Walcie had just put a plate of biscuits on the table when Red walked to the door, paused for a moment with his hand on the knob and said, "I'll be back in a little while." A little while turned into a fortnight and that was when Walcie received a postcard from him, saying he would be back soon. On the front of the card was a picture of the Gulf of Mexico from Galveston harbor.

JAMES A. OWEN HAD moved to Seminole, Oklahoma, in the 1920s, a time when the town was beginning a transformation from a mostly agricultural, mostly poor town into one of the largest oil suppliers in the world. With the oil boom came thousands of people looking for good jobs and good times. Riggers worked hard and partied hard and earned the name that became part of American slang: roughnecks. Prostitutes, gamblers, dope peddlers and other nefarious sorts descended on Seminole. One bootleg business operated from a taxi company that was within full view of the city's police department. Police Chief Jake Sims had other priorities. He also had a strange power over denizens of the underworld. Slightly built—a welterweight in boxing jargon—he never wore a gun but nonetheless had the respect of all manner of crooks. Reporters said he could take down men twice his size with nothing but a scolding. Instead of locking up shoplifters, he asked them to return the stolen goods, and the thieves complied. A hooker who had only half the money to pay a fine for plying her trade was released so she could "earn" the rest. Bribes and kickbacks were part of the system, but Seminole's honest citizens looked the other way because in exchange for leniency in petty wrongdoings, Jake Sims had eyes and ears keeping him abreast of much more serious criminal activity in Seminole. In 1932, he took part in the search for Pretty Boy Floyd after Floyd robbed the Bank of Seminole. Sims was a dogged detective when it came to the vilest offenses. Murderers beware.

By the end of 1940, Seminole's population explosion had ebbed, as had the flow of black gold, but oil remained a critical part of the town's existence with pump stations, refineries, distributors and other oil-related businesses remaining there. James Owen, who had been with the Cities Service Company for over twenty years, stayed on as the chief warehouseman for the Lacey Lease.

The sixty-two-year-old Owen and his wife, Lillie May, had three daughters, two of whom wanted to do some shopping a couple of days before Christmas in 1940. Their father dropped them off downtown that evening after he got off work. Stores were all decked out for the holidays with glittering lights, angel hair, gold and silver tinsel and garlands of green with red velvet bows. Windows showed off favorite seasonal gift choices: dolls, model train sets, cashmere sweaters, camel hair coats and the latest in millinery accessories. Drugstores, such as the Parks on Main Street, offered boxed candy and, for those thirsty from buying presents, cokes and malts at the soda fountain.

After letting the girls out, Owen did a little shopping of his own and asked the sale clerks to wrap the presents in paper adorned with whimsical patterns: snowmen, candy canes and Santa Claus. Putting the bundles in the back seat, he drove around and parked alongside the International Derrick and Equipment Company just south of the Rock Island tracks on First Street. Then he joined six friends for a two-bit poker game in the Ideco Drilling Supplies Building. The game broke up about 9:00 p.m., and Owen's pals left him standing by his car. He had lost about four dollars but still had around fifty in his wallet. An hour and a half later, after a short search, his daughters saw the car and opened the backseat door to load their packages. For a flash of a second when the dome light came on, it looked as if all the gifts already in the car were wrapped in shiny, red foil. It was only after they saw their father slumped over the steering wheel that reality hit them. Blood was everywhere. Owen's head had been beaten so forcefully shards of his skull stuck out like pieces of a broken china bowl filled with pureed strawberries.

Owen's daughters became hysterical and fled screaming from the grisly sight. The first people to come to their aid had difficulty understanding what they were trying to say, but they were able to lead the way to their father. Afterward, the young ladies were hospitalized for shock.

The killer or killers had struck the victim on his head at least twenty times with a fourteen-inch iron rig brace found at the scene. The assistant district attorney believed the motive was robbery because the fifty dollars was missing from Owen's pockets. About fifteen men were considered serious suspects, but by the end of January, all had been released from custody. The best fingerprint expert with the State Department of Public Safety in Oklahoma City could not find any usable prints on the blood-smeared iron bar because of its rough, grooved surface. During his tenure as police chief, Jake Sims was instrumental in the capture of at least fifty murderers, but the slayer of Jim Owen wasn't one of them.

WALCIE LONGED FOR HER husband but put on a brave face for her mother. Amanda got into the Yuletide spirit and helped her daughter decorate the house with pinecones and holly. They gathered pecans from a nearby grove and bought apples and oranges from Lasley's Grocery and Feed Store at the crossroads in Enola. The two women always baked a lot for Christmas, and guests partook of cookies, cakes and pies made from old family recipes. The fragrance of nature and sweets were treats for the olfactory senses.

Then on Christmas Day, like a sleighless Santa Claus, Red came home. Walcie was both relieved and angry.

"I've been beside myself with worry," she said. "Where in the world were you?"

He shrugged. "No place special. Didn't you get my card?"

"Yes, but you can't just up and leave like that."

Red hung his head under the reprimand but cheered up when he remembered the package concealed under his coat.

"Here," he said, giving the brown paper bundle to Walcie.

"What's this?" she asked.

"It's your Christmas present. Go on. Open it."

She untied the string that held the package together. Inside was a bolt of brocade fabric with silver threads woven through a paisley pattern of burgundy and black.

"I bought it in Fort Smith," he said. "Should be enough there to make dresses for you and your mother both."

"It's beautiful, Red." Walcie caressed the material. "But you shouldn't have."

"And here," he said, pulling a small brown bag out of his coat pocket and showing her the contents: hard candy in all colors and flavors.

Though Walcie forgave her husband, his road trip left her with an uneasy feeling that he would abandon her again, an intuition that was prophetic. The following summer, when she was expecting their first child and their crop was coming up, he told her he was going into town.

"I don't think you have any business going to town," she said.

"Now don't you worry," he soothed her and kissed her goodbye.

He didn't come back that night nor the next day, and Walcie realized she and her mother were on their own once more. Tearfully, she went to her in-laws and asked them for help in carrying on with the crops. Red's father and brother Lawrence stepped in to fill the shoes of the absent husband. Ten days after Red's disappearing act, Walcie got a card from him to let her know he was okay, but it was nearly a month more before he returned home. Walcie was glad to see him but naturally upset and asked him why he had deserted her.

"I didn't desert you," he said. "I'm back."

"Well, why did you go in the first place? Are you dissatisfied with me?"

"I just needed to get away for a while," he said.

"But I'm your wife. Your place is here with me and your unborn child."

A contrite Red was in the doghouse for a short time, but he and Walcie carried on as they prepared to welcome a new life into the world. On Christmas Day 1941, they sent for Dr. E.M. Ingram. It was a difficult delivery. The baby was in a breech position, and Walcie was in great pain. Red was sitting on a sofa when Ingram came out of the bedroom and told him the baby wouldn't live. The news caused Red to fall on the floor in a convulsion, but he soon regained his senses and got back up without help. By then, the baby was dead.

The disappointed couple tried to put the trauma behind them. Walcie suffered no lasting physical effects from her ordeal, and Red was attentive and supportive. By spring, however, moss was growing under his feet, and Walcie recognized the restless look on his face.

"I feel like something's drawing you away from me," she said, crying.

Red started crying, too, and told her he was leaving, bound for Louisiana. Not even Red himself knew what compelled him to go. He just started hiking down the road and was still crying when he passed Lasley's Store. Then, five or six weeks later, he was back home again.

Amanda was none too happy with her son-in-law's lack of ambition. She could only hope for the best when the three of them moved to England, Arkansas, to sharecrop. Red ran the tractor and, with his wife, hoed cotton. It was hot, dirty work. The flat fields were beautiful in spring with white flowering cotton turning to pink after pollination. And in late summer and early fall, big, fluffy puffs of cotton draped the landscape like reflections of the billowy white cumulus clouds in the sky. But for the people who toiled there, it was sometimes hard to see the beauty around them. With the sun beating down and temperatures of ninety degrees or higher, chopping weeds and picking cotton could age a person quickly. Men wore wide-brimmed hats, and women shaded their faces with bonnets, but sweat rolled down out from under the headgear and left beads of grime in the creases of their necks. It would be another decade before mechanical cotton-pickers rolled into the Arkansas fields.

Red soon tired of the backbreaking work. The landowner wanted the Halls to work longer hours, from sunup to sundown, but Red refused. He exchanged words with the man, the upshot being that the Halls moved to Little Rock, where Red found employment as a taxi driver for the Yellow and Checker Cab Company. He didn't work there steadily but returned several times over the next three years. Walcie got a job with the Jackson Cookie Company in North Little Rock and later with Colonial Bakery.

On May 11, 1943, Walcie had another baby, a healthy son. She hoped fatherhood would make Red more responsible, but that prospect never entered his mind. He continued to roam, staying away for weeks at a time. Finally, Walcie decided she'd had enough and left, but it was Red who actually asked for a divorce.

"It's nothing against you," he told her, "But I don't like your mother living with us. She's always sticking her nose in where it don't belong."

After the divorce, Red was always punctual in paying Walcie ten dollars a month toward the support of their son.

Red was officially footloose and fancy free, but he couldn't take advantage of the situation to go on an extended tour of the United States because he had managed to stay put in one place long enough for the U.S. Navy to find him. Though many men had donned the bell-bottom trousers to keep from being drafted into the army or marines, by 1943, the government needed about ten million more men for the war effort. The navy began conscripting able-bodied men, and Red was one of them, inducted on October 19, 1943. His military career was short-lived, however, when he exhibited an inability to follow orders. After only six weeks, his superiors at the Navy Training Station told him he was being discharged because of "indifference." He didn't know what that meant but figured it was the navy's loss.

FAYRENE CLEMMONS WAS THE daughter of A.Z. and Ada Clemmons, who owned a farm south of Lonoke, Arkansas, on Star Route 31. Fay was a healthy girl and attractive in her own way. Like her father, she had a lower tooth that overlapped another, and some folks called her bucktoothed, but she didn't mind. She took good care of her teeth and smiled and laughed wholeheartedly. She was well-adjusted and asserted her independence when she was seventeen years old by moving to Little Rock. Staying under the protective eye of her family, she lived with her half brother William "Bill" A. Stevenson, and his wife, Muriel. She and Muriel had been friends since 1939,

Fayrene Clemmons Hall.
Illustration by Wyatt Jones.

before they became in-laws. They corresponded with each other when Fay stretched her wings a little more and moved to St. Louis, where she got a job as a restaurant cashier. She returned to Little Rock sometime around December 1943, and soon after that, she met Red Hall. It was a whirlwind courtship, for they married in March 1944. If only they had dated longer, Fay could have seen more of Red's dark side. It might have saved her life.

3

HATE AND MARRIAGE

I t didn't take Red long to see how different his second wife was from his first. Fay was feistier and more adventurous than Walcie, and when Red wanted to go traveling about, Fay wanted to go, too, but he didn't take to the notion. Eventually, after a fuss, he would agree and allow her to accompany him, and on one trip they went to Oregon. Fay sent her parents two letters and a postcard from there. She always stayed in touch with her family, no matter where she was. Red wondered if he could trust such a headstrong wife. He also thought she fooled away too much money on pretty clothes and such. They quarreled about that, among other things. She tried to hold her own against his explosive temper, but he punctuated his side of an argument with a fist to her face.

A.Z. and Ada didn't meet Red Hall until after he was already married to their daughter. A.Z.'s first impression of Red was positive. "He made a fine appearance and had a wonderful personality," Clemmons later said. "Until you knew him and found the devil way back in him."

Ada Clemmons began to doubt her new son-in-law after the first time Fay came home covered with bruises. Red was with her.

"What happened to you?" she asked Fay, but Red was the one who answered.

"Aw, we were just scuffling, having some fun," he laughed it off.

Ima Gean often saw her sister Fay black and blue.

"Red's jealous and always accusing Fay of looking at other men," Ima Gean told her parents. "He's well aware that she's never paid attention to another since they've been married."

"I know," Ada said. "Several times he's admitted to me that Fay gives him no reason to be jealous."

Ada thought Red was just plain mean and told her husband so.

"He nags Fay over the least little thing and keeps on for hours. Even the most pleasant girl can't stand that forever."

Ada was right. In the summer of '44, Fay told her father, "I can't make it much longer with Red."

ON AUGUST 22, 1944, Wehman J. Peacock Jr. kissed his wife goodbye and left Oklahoma City for Joplin, Missouri, to visit his parents. Ten days later, when he should have been back home safe and sound, he wasn't, so his wife alerted authorities. The following week, police found his black 1940 Ford Deluxe Tudor parked in front of a hotel in Pittsburg, Kansas, but Peacock was nowhere to be seen.

At the time of his disappearance, he was an insurance adjuster for Horton Claims Service in Oklahoma City's Hightower Building, and detectives wondered if he might have been a victim of foul play at the hands of someone he had been investigating. His wife hoped that if he had been hurt, perhaps he was suffering from amnesia and just couldn't find his way home. Then on October 18, a farmer walking along the roadside south of Miami, Oklahoma, discovered a body among high weeds in a ditch. The skull, totally devoid of flesh or skin, was separated from the body. The Oklahoma State Patrol identified the deceased as Peacock after his wife provided them with dental records that matched the teeth in the skull.

As for the gross condition of the corpse, one had to take into account the body's exposure to the elements for over a month. Even though decomposition was advanced, the coroner easily determined the cause of death as a bullet to the head. A strange aspect to the slaying was the fact that the victim was dressed in someone else's clothes. When last seen alive, Peacock was wearing nice, somewhat expensive garments. The apparel on his remains consisted of a shirt without a necktie, plain khaki pants with a tan sport coat and simple brown Oxford shoes. A straw hat was on the ground nearby. Ottawa County sheriff Dee Watters speculated that a hitchhiker had robbed and killed Peacock. Watters said a spate of hitchhike-related crimes had occurred in his jurisdiction in recent memory.

The 555 Building was a familiar landmark to Little Rock residents and to out-of-towners who often visited the capital city. Opened in 1917, the 555 Tire and Service Company was the brainchild of Roy Edward Stueber, who had recognized the need for such a business when automobiles began to replace the horse and wagon as America's preferred mode of transportation. Once billed as the largest service station in the world, standing four stories high, the 555 was strategically located at the corner of Third and Broadway, a particularly busy intersection since Broadway Street was also part of US 67. Steuber named the structure after its easily remembered telephone number. A vintage Ford roadster was the eye-catching crowning glory displayed atop the building, where an American flag flew over the conspicuously large numerals. The second and third floors were rented out as a storage space for cars, but the top floor was the unlikely site of a popular ballroom, the Rainbow Garden. A Tiffany crystal chandelier illuminated the nightspot, which could accommodate as many as five hundred dancers, all swaying to the romantic rhythms of "Bésame Mucho" by Jimmy Dorsey or jazzing it up to the live orchestral tunes of the "Hi-De-Ho Man" himself, Cab Calloway.

The 555 Building, home of the Rainbow Garden ballroom. *Courtesy UA Little Rock Center for Arkansas History and Culture.*

Fay loved the Rainbow Garden, thought it was positively magical. Sometimes Red went with her, but she never knew if he would stay or just drop her off and pick her up later. Either was fine with her. His quicksilver moods could spoil any occasion. Besides, she didn't need him to have a good time. She had made new friends, including a woman named Dorothy Barton, who also liked to dance.

In July, not long after she met Dorothy, Fay left Red and moved in with her new pal, whose husband was away at the time. The ladies enjoyed going to the movies and frequented the Rex Theatre on Main Street. A few doors up from there was another theater called the Roxy, but the Rex was air-conditioned, so it was their favorite. They roomed together for about three weeks, and then Fay decided to give her marriage another try and went back to Red. On August 25, 1944, the two of them rented a four-room apartment from W.A. Woods, who owned and operated a neighborhood grocery store with living quarters at 3223 Maryland Avenue in Little Rock. Red and Fay had been Woods's customers before becoming his tenants. The ersatz love nest consisted of a living room, kitchen, bedroom and bathroom.

On Sunday, September 10, 1944, Muriel Stevenson went to the Halls' apartment. Red wasn't there, and in his absence, the two women had a good visit. Fay modeled a new two-piece red dress and was wearing a pair of shoes she had bought during a recent shopping trip with Muriel.

"I love that dress," Muriel said, "Especially the buttons. They're so unusual."

Each button had a chain attached to it, and at the chain's end was a thin metallic strip that looked like a tiny sword, which slipped into a slot in the button.

"Yeah, but these shoes hurt my feet," Fay said. "I haven't broken them in yet."

When Red came home, Muriel said goodbye to Fay and left.

The next day, when Fay went to her parents' farm, she was in high spirits and relished the big chicken supper that her mother had fixed.

The following Thursday, September 14, Fay called a friend named Katherine "Katy" Bryant, extending an invitation to go to the Rainbow Garden with her and Red that night.

"It's Ladies Night," she said.

"Sure, I'll go," Katy accepted, "But you'll have to pick me up."

Katy worked at a café for a Mrs. Lancaster in the 1100 block of Markham, and it was from there that Fay and Red gave her a ride to the nightclub. Entertainment that evening included music by a local band, a variety show and then more dance tunes. The trio stayed until midnight, and then, as they were leaving, Red and Fay began sniping at each other. She wanted to ride the elevator down because her feet were killing her, but Red insisted they take the stairs. She continued to complain, and he grabbed her and shook her so hard she lost one of her shoes. When she stopped to pick it up, he jerked her by the elbow.

"How much did them shoes cost?" he asked. "You can't even wear 'em. And that fancy dress. You had plenty of dresses."

Disdainfully, he toyed with the edge of Fay's collar and then yanked it, a motion that partially unbuttoned the dress. Katy hurriedly helped her refasten the distinctive closure.

The car was parked up the street, and as Fay got into it, she said, "Red Hall, I won't live with you."

He rebuked her with a stinging slap to her face. She drew a hand up to repel another blow, but none came. Red was walking around to the driver's side. Fay scooted over on the car seat to make room for Katy, who was anxious to get home and out of the uncomfortable situation in which she found herself.

On the way, Fay announced, "I'm leaving and going to the coast."

Red was infuriated and stepped on the gas, flying right past Katy's house on Second Street.

"Red, I want out at home," she said.

He made a screeching hairpin U-turn and sped back down the street, parking across from Katy's house. As she exited the vehicle, she said an awkward "Goodnight." That was the last time she ever saw Fay.

The next morning, Muriel called Fay, but Red answered the phone and said Fay had left him the night before.

On Sunday, September 17, three of Fay's cousins drove up from Pine Bluff to see her but learned from Red that she had been gone for three days. They reported this to Fay's parents, who drove to Little Rock to look for her. Red was gone, and they couldn't find their daughter, though her clothes were still in the apartment. They didn't contact the police right away, hoping that Fay had left Red and that she would show up at the farm any moment. But she didn't.

Ten days after Fay's disappearance, Ada and Ima Gean went to the Little Rock Police Department and talked to Chief of Detectives O.N. Martin. Though Martin had been a cop for twenty-seven years, he carried himself with the banty rooster strut of some of his favorite movie gangsters. It was easy to picture him as a pugilistic Irishman from the streets of New York with his rosy complexion that grew redder when he was excited and a ready smile that could turn into a sneer at the drop of his fedora.

"What seems to be your problem, ma'am?" Martin asked.

"My daughter Fay is missing," Ada said, "And I know something is wrong."

"OK. Sit down and tell me about it." He reached for a missing person's report and a pencil. "What's your name, ma'am, and where do you live?"

"Mrs. A.Z. Clemmons, Ada Clemmons. And this is Fay's sister, Ima Gean. I'm from Lonoke."

"Well, I'm afraid that's outside of my jurisdiction," Martin said, laying the paper down on his desk.

"Oh, wait." Ada opened her purse and retrieved a card with a note written on it. "I went to our sheriff, and he told me to give this to you."

Martin took the card and read the short message that introduced Ada.

"He said I should talk to you because Fay lived here in Little Rock."

"I understand. Do you have a picture of her? That would be helpful."

"I do." Ada retrieved a snapshot of Fay from her purse and gave it to Martin. "And her name is Fay?"

"Fayrene Hall. We call her Fay."

"You say her last name is Hall? She's married?" Martin asked, taking down the information as it was given to him.

"Yes, her husband is James Waybern Hall, but everybody calls him 'Red' because he has red hair."

"He's roughed Fay up more than once," Ima Gean said.

"What does he say about Fay's whereabouts?" Martin asked.

"I can't get hold of him. He's never at home."

"Well, where does he work?"

"He drives a taxi for the Yellow and Checker Cab Company, but I can't ever catch him there either. I've left messages for him, but he's not very dependable, if you know what I mean."

"What *do* you mean?"

"He skips from job to job a lot. His father's a preacher, but you'd never know it by the way Red acts. My husband and I didn't meet him until after he and Fay were already married."

"And when was that?"

"March of this year."

"You say he's roughed her up?"

"Yes, sir. He hits her sometimes. She left him for a little while earlier this summer but went back to him."

"Do you think maybe she's just left him again?"

"No." Ada was emphatic. "My nieces found out she was missing ten days ago, but I waited 'til today to see you because I thought she might have been hiding from Red. She wouldn't have been gone this long, though. Not without letting any of her family know. And besides that, when I went by their place, all of her clothes were still there."

Ada and Ima Gean left after answering all the questions posed by Martin, who assigned the case to Detectives Harold Judd and Herbert A. Peterson.

Judd and Peterson worked well as a team. Judd, a veteran detective of twenty-three years, sported a neatly trimmed moustache and an affable demeanor. Peterson, a member of the LRPD going on nineteen years, had a way of looking at suspects as if his eyes were lie detectors always probing for the truth.

The two men drove to the Yellow and Checker Cab Company to see if they would have more luck finding Red Hall than his mother-in-law had. He was out when they got there, but as they waited for his return, they interviewed Fred Vernan, the cab company manager.

"As long as he's worked here, Red's been a nice boy," Vernan said. "I'm always glad to talk to him and listen to his troubles. He doesn't work steadily. He goes off and travels about, I think, but we've always welcomed him back. He's a good cab driver, a very smart driver. A little rough on equipment, maybe."

When Red drove up, he knew Peterson and Judd were cops even though they were in plain clothes. He'd been expecting them and couldn't shrug them off the way he had his in-laws. He kept his cool and didn't let their presence fluster him. He told them about going to the Rainbow Garden with Fay and Katy Bryant. He owned up to slapping Fay during an argument. How could he lie about it? They would get around to Katy eventually.

"What happened after you dropped Miss Bryant off?" Peterson asked.

"We went home, and I laid down on the bed and listened to the radio. Fay went in the bathroom, and she was in there so long, I got worried about her and went to look for her. I went through the bathroom and living room and on out to the car, but I didn't see her anywhere, so I went back to bed."

"Your wife disappears, and you go to sleep?" Peterson asked.

"Well, what was I supposed to do? We'd had words, and she said she was leaving me to go to the coast."

"The coast?" Judd tilted his head. "Which coast?"

"California," Red answered. "She's always wanted to go to California. Ask her mother."

"And you haven't heard from her?" Peterson asked.

"Nope," Red replied, adding, "Fay was fine the last time I saw her."

After Ada got home from Little Rock, she changed clothes and went to work in the garden. When she straightened up to stretch her back a bit, she saw Red Hall coming her way through the turn row.

"Red, where have you been and where's Fay?" she asked.

"She left me," he said.

"Well, have you heard from her?"

"No, I haven't."

Strands of brown hair strayed from under Ada's bonnet. Her sun-squinted eyes looked hard at her son-in-law as she asked him, "Red, have you had trouble?"

"Yes, we've had a fight," he confessed.

"Did you hurt her?"

"No, not bad, I don't think," he said. "She left me after we went dancing one night."

"Have you seen the law?"

"This morning."

"You going to see them anymore?"

"Yes, I expect I better," he replied.

When Ada informed her husband about the encounter, he gave up hope. He later told newspaper reporters, "I could tell then in my own mind that she was gone, but there was nothing I could do."

Three days after his first trip to the Clemmons farm, Red drove out there again and brought Fay's clothes. He asked Ada if she had been to see the detectives again.

"I certainly have," she said. "And if I live twenty-five years more and don't find her, I'll keep going to 'em."

"Look, if it'll make you feel any better, come with me, and we'll look for her together."

"I'm not about to go anywhere with you," Ada said.

"Suit yourself then," and Red left.

Ada suspected that if she had taken Red up on his offer to accompany her in her search, he would see to it that she disappeared, too. In the following weeks and months, she continued to look for Fay on her own and also checked with the detectives frequently. Red carried on with his life, coming and going as he pleased without the worry of a wife. He moved out of the Maryland Avenue apartment and, in late 1944, he traveled west along the roads and highways he knew so well.

ON FRIDAY, NOVEMBER 3, 1944, newspapers in Kansas reported the discovery of two deceased men lying in a weed-covered ditch off a lightly traveled road near Moundbridge in McPherson County. Both had suffered fatal gunshot wounds. One of the men was Dr. Merrill E. Lambert, a thirty-five-year-old osteopath from Canton, Kansas, who had been missing for four days. A picture that ran with the story showed Lambert was a handsome, dapper-looking man. The other victim was Corporal Charles W. Nipper III. Corporal Nipper was part of the 247th Army Airfield Force and had been hitchhiking back to his base unit at Smoky Hill AAF in Salina, Kansas.

Kansas State Highway Patrolmen Glenn Boden and Donald Ford spotted the bodies five miles north of Hesston and a half mile west of the Canton-Hesston Road. It looked as if the killer had dragged the victims into the ditch by their coat collars. Both men's wallets were missing, although jewelry, including the doctor's wristwatch, were not taken, and the soldier was still wearing his dog tags, so the murderer hadn't attempted to remove identification, or he may have been interrupted before he could.

McPherson County coroner Dr. A.M. Lorentz said Lambert bore three bullet wounds near the right shoulder blade. Nipper, too, was shot near the right shoulder blade but also sustained wounds in the right hand and left jaw. Lorentz said no inquest would be held, that both men were victims of "cold-blooded murder."

Peace officers from four counties and volunteer posses had been scouring the countryside between Wichita and Canton ever since Lambert's black Buick sedan was found near a cabin camp on US 81. Bloodstains were on the front seat, the running board and the inside of the rear bumper. Detective Don Finney, a laboratory technician with the Wichita Police Department, inspected the car and said a bullet hole was in the upholstery on the left door panel.

Lambert had taken a patient to the Southwestern Osteopathic Hospital in Wichita and left there shortly after 8:00 p.m. on the Monday preceding discovery of the bodies. He picked up Nipper at a roadside shelter at Twenty-First Street and Broadway in Wichita, where Virginia Clanton told police she had seen Nipper enter a car similar to Lambert's. The slayings prompted an editorial in the *Wichita Daily Beacon* that read:

> *The tragic, untimely, and unnecessary deaths of the doctor and the soldier were due to the non-enforcement of the Kansas law against hitchhiking. It is a violation of a Kansas statute for a motor driver to pick up a hitchhiker. It is a violation of the law for any person to solicit a ride by the "thumbing" method. At no time since its passage years ago has the law against hitchhiking*

been enforced. Yet there have been numerous cold-blooded murders by persons given free rides by Kansas motorists. In spite of the law against picking up hitchhikers and in the face of the accumulation of brutal murders, nobody is prosecuted—either motor drivers or hitchhikers—for the flagrant and deadly law violations.

After visiting California for a short while, Red hitchhiked across the country again, taking the southern route back home. When he returned to Little Rock, he was driving a maroon Chevrolet with a Texas license plate and a load of Bibles in the back seat. A service station operator asked him why he had so many Bibles, and Hall said he was selling them for a company based in Dallas, Texas.

Also in December 1944, Katy Bryant received a Christmas card from Fayrene. The envelope was postmarked Bakersfield, California. The greetings read in part, "Please tell Mom and all that it's really great out here and I soon will feel settled and will write. Do you see Red around?"

Bryant contacted the Clemmonses who, in turn, called Chief Martin. Peterson and Judd went to get the card from Bryant, but they were too late. Red had already been there and gone, taking the Christmas card and envelope with him. Following the trail, the detectives found Hall, but he didn't have the card on him. He promised to bring it and the envelope to them at the police station but never did. Bryant couldn't authenticate the handwriting because she wasn't familiar with Fay's. They had never corresponded, and she soon forgot what it had looked like on the card.

The holiday season was grim for the Clemmons family, the empty chair at the dinner table a reminder of their loss, for they knew they would never see their beloved Fay again.

4

THE HITCHHIKE KILLER

Around 8:00 a.m. on Wednesday, January 17, 1945, while working with a timber crew, Girvis Haltom discovered the bloody body of a man slumped against the base of a tree just outside of Camden near the Fairview Cut-off Highway in Ouachita County. Upon inspection, some of the lumbermen recognized the victim as Carl Hamilton, a local barber and bootlegger. No fewer than eleven liquor stores were located near Camden's ordnance plant, but bootleggers still kept plenty busy. Hamilton had been shot to death. An autopsy revealed two .45-caliber bullet wounds, one in the side and one in the heart. The coroner put the time of death around midnight. Because many soldiers carried .45-caliber side arms, the Ouachita County Sheriff's Office theorized the killer might have been a serviceman. Any crime involving a member of the armed forces meant the sheriff could request assistance from the Arkansas State Police (ASP), and that is what he did.

The Arkansas state legislature created the ASP in 1935. Until then, there had been no law enforcement agency that covered all seventy-five counties of the Wonder State, as Arkansas was called at that time. Local sheriffs and constables had traditionally resisted relinquishing any power to a central organization, but they changed their tune for several reasons: a rise in the number of vehicular accidents and deaths, enforcement of new liquor laws following the end of Prohibition and the fact that criminals were more mobile in the age of the automobile. After only two years, the force expanded to fifty-five districts, or troops, around the state.

J. Earl Scroggin was a member of the original thirteen troopers or "rangers," as they were termed initially. Before that, he spent ten years as a motorcycle patrolman with the North Little Rock Police Department; it was during that time that he suffered serious injuries in a traffic accident, something he considered a minor setback. It didn't prevent him from rising quickly in the ranks of the rangers. He had a spotless reputation and was an expert in identification techniques such as fingerprint analysis, and by 1945, he was Captain Scroggin, based at Troop One in Little Rock. Slender, balding and soft-spoken, he could have been mistaken for an

Captain J. Earl Scroggin. *Courtesy Steven A. Coppinger.*

accountant. When he received word of the Hamilton slaying, he assigned the case to Lieutenant Rhett Oliphant and Sergeant Homer Sims. They talked to Hamilton's sister, who said he had left his home in Camden about 8:30 p.m., but she didn't know where he had gone. She also said he often carried large sums of money. The victim's pockets had been turned inside out and his shoes removed. Even though robbery was considered to be the motive, sheriff's deputies had found a little over three dollars in cash on the body along with a watch, a fraternal ring and a pocketknife.

Hamilton's murder reaped a skimpy newspaper notice of only two short paragraphs. The war was a natural distraction and led the news every day. Print space about murders, suicides and other such tragedies was kept to a minimum. But the report of Hamilton's untimely death was brief for another reason—his race. Hamilton was Black, and it was the era of the Jim Crow laws, which were intended to keep the races segregated. The term *Jim Crow* itself was a derisive epithet left over from minstrel shows. Newspapers made the distinction between whites and Black citizens, always inserting the word "Negro" when items were about African Americans. Obituaries had a section called "Deaths of Negroes," and those, when printed at all, merited only three to five lines, unless the deceased was prominent in the community. Hamilton's was slightly longer because he died at the hands of another person.

RED'S CABBIE CAREER CONTINUED intermittently, but whenever he took a notion to go somewhere, he just up and went. He was beholden to no one and responsible for only himself. On February 1, 1945, he decided to hitch a ride south. He knew the odds of someone stopping for him were especially good on that day because it had been raining off and on, and the temperature was in the thirties after an overnight low of twenty-five degrees. If his smile didn't convince a driver to stop, his huddled, shivering figure would do the trick, and he was right. It didn't take long. Pity fosters kindness, and near the viaduct at the corner of Thirty-Third and Arch Streets in Little Rock, a Studebaker sedan slowed and then stopped. Red opened the passenger door and stuck his head inside. A well-groomed, bespectacled, middle-aged man was behind the wheel.

"Where you headed?" the man asked.

"Louisiana," Red answered.

"Well, I can take you as far as Camden."

"That'll do." Red hopped in. "Much obliged to you, Mister."

"I'm E.C. Adams," the driver said.

"James Hall."

The two shook hands and were off.

Later that day, around 4:30 p.m., Edgar McCollum, a country store proprietor and part-time deputy sheriff, noticed a car with Kansas plates parked by the roadside about fourteen miles north of Fordyce on US 167. He didn't see anyone in or near the car as he passed by. On his return trip ninety minutes later, the vehicle was still there, so he stopped to take a look. It appeared someone had unsuccessfully tried to start the car without a key by wiring the ignition, and the interior of the Studebaker had been rifled. The glove compartment was open, and maps, several insurance policies and other papers were spread out on the seat. McCollum also saw tools and a small hatchet with what appeared to be bloodstains on it. He spied two sets of shoe prints on the ground leading off into the woods, but only one set led back to the highway. Following the tracks to an area of dense trees and undergrowth, the deputy found the body of a man lying face-down on a brittle bed of frosty, dead leaves, his head plastered with blood.

McCollum hurried back to his store three miles away and notified Cleveland County sheriff T.H. Glover and the state police. Captain Scroggin and Detectives Oliphant and Sims sped to the crime scene about eighty miles south of Little Rock. Also responding were Camden patrolman Buchanan and ASP sergeant Copeland.

The victim's pockets were turned inside out, his shoes and socks had been taken off his feet and an empty wallet with the initials ECA lay beside him. A closer examination of the body revealed a set of car keys in a small hidden pocket of the man's coat. A trace of the license plate identified the car as belonging to E.C. Adams of Humboldt, Kansas. When authorities notified his wife, Marian Adams, she couldn't believe the dead man was her husband.

"It can't be him," she cried. "It mustn't be him. We have a two-week-old baby."

After pulling herself together as best she could, the bereaved widow was able to answer some questions posed by investigators. Her husband was a skilled mechanic and carpenter who had worked in a defense plant in California before moving to Kansas. The day before he was killed, he had kissed her and their infant daughter goodbye to begin the drive to Camden, where he had found new employment at the naval ordnance plant there. His family was to join him later.

Mrs. Adams gave police a list of items her husband had taken with him. They included clothing, several cartons of cigarettes, a razor, a shaving mug, razor blades, traveler's checks and a small amount of cash. All of these things were missing. Also gone were two alarm clocks. Adams was an unusually sound sleeper and had packed a brown spring-driven alarm clock and a newer electric clock. The older clock's case had been marred by a cigarette burn. Adams had a couple of watches, too: an elaborately engraved white gold hexagonal Waltham and an Elgin in a silver case.

Contrary to first reports, the hatchet in Adams's car wasn't the murder weapon. The blood on the hatchet wasn't even human. The coroner pronounced the cause of death as a gunshot wound to the back of the head, and ASP ballistics expert Alan Templeton determined the slug was a .38 caliber.

After the autopsy, Adams's family made arrangements to take his body to his native home, Des Moines, Iowa, for burial. Besides his wife and baby, he was survived by another daughter from a previous marriage, a stepson and two sisters.

Back in Arkansas, the search for the killer continued. Owing to the proximity, both in time and location, to the Hamilton slaying and the suspected motive of robbery in the two cases, Scroggin wondered if they were committed by the same person, possibly a hitchhiker. Adams's family didn't agree with the theory because he had been robbed once before when he gave a man a lift. It just didn't figure that he would take such a risk again.

Detectives Oliphant and Sims backtracked the route Adams had driven from Humboldt, checking with hotels and tourist court managers along US 64 through Muskogee, Oklahoma, and on to Fort Smith, where he stopped over on Wednesday night. According to sales receipts recovered from the victim's belongings, he had bought a pair of overalls and white duck cloth from two stores in Little Rock on Thursday morning. Nobody at either store remembered seeing anyone with him. Thinking Adams wouldn't have made any more stops after leaving the capital city, investigators deduced that if he had picked up someone, he did so in Little Rock. Therefore, Scroggin alerted Detective Chief Martin at the LRPD.

ONE WEEK AFTER THE Adams murder, thirty-year-old Doyle Mulherin was going about his routine as a truck driver for the Western Meat Company, and if anybody stuck to a routine, it was Mulherin. People along his route between Little Rock and Stuttgart could set their watches by him. That's why store proprietors became concerned when he failed to appear with their orders. A call to his employer verified that he had left Little Rock at eight o'clock that Friday morning, and further investigation confirmed he had made deliveries and collections as far as the little town of Brummitt. He left there at 12:15 p.m., after stopping at the M.E. Temple Store about seven miles from his final destination of Stuttgart. A search was conducted, and shortly after 6:00 p.m., grocer and Stuttgart mayor Harley Stump found Mulherin's abandoned truck on the outskirts of town. It wasn't until the next day, however, that two fishermen discovered Mulherin's body in a ditch about twenty-five feet from the highway near the Bayou Meto Bridge.

Prairie County sheriff E.O. Hamilton called the ASP, and at the behest of Captain Scroggin, Detectives Oliphant and Sims responded. They soon saw similarities between the slayings of Mulherin and Adams. According to the meat company, Mulherin had made enough deliveries and collected enough payments to fill three wallets, but his pockets had been turned wrong side out and no wallet was found. He had also been shot in the back of the head. Then came the clincher. After the medical examiner dug a .38-caliber slug out of the victim's skull, Templeton's ballistics test showed the bullets that killed Adams and Mulherin came from the same gun.

The Mulherin murder was one of the killer's most profitable, garnering him $129, but it would also prove to be the one that gave detectives their first big break in the series of slayings. Mulherin had been known by people along his route, and they remembered seeing him in the truck with another man.

While retracing Mulherin's movements on his last day of work, Detectives Oliphant and Sims talked to Clarence Fugate, a truck driver whose route ran in the opposite direction of Mulherin's. The two men usually waved when they passed each other. On the day in question, however, Mulherin had a passenger with him and didn't seem to notice his fellow trucker. Fugate described the passenger as a young man with wavy red hair. Coincidentally, Fugate's father lived along his son's route and went out to the highway to flag Clarence down for a ride into town. While he waited, the elder Fugate saw the familiar Western Meat truck and noticed the driver had someone with him. The police talked to the Fugates separately, yet each one told the same thing and gave the same description of the passenger: a youth with red hair. Then two boys who had been fishing in Bayou Meto said they had seen a man loitering near the bridge around the time of the murder, a good-looking young fellow with wavy red hair. This was the first tangible clue to the identity of the murderer soon to be called the Hitchhike Killer.

5

END OF THE LINE

On Friday, March 2, 1945, authorities were called to break up a fight in a back alley behind a bar and grill near Second and Center Streets in Little Rock. By the time they arrived, however, the fight was over. A burly young man was lying unconscious on the ground, while the other combatant stood victorious with nary a scratch or bruise on him. Lean but muscular, with blue eyes and red hair, he gave his name as Jim "Red" Hall. The loser in the alley brawl, William Blevins, was beaten and stomped so savagely that he was hospitalized and on the critical list for thirty-six hours. Even after his condition improved, he remained in the hospital for several weeks.

Hall pleaded guilty to simple assault and was let off with a fine of $100 plus $6.90 in court costs. Talking his way out of jail time by claiming self-defense, he also mentioned to the judge that he was a navy veteran and the son of a minister. Sometimes, especially when he was in the company of young ladies, Red alluded to his participation in the Battles of Midway and Guadalcanal. If the men who gave him rides ever wondered aloud why their passenger wasn't still in the service, they may have triggered an angry response that brought on their hasty demise.

Unlike Hall's cavalier attitude toward the war, most people anxiously checked newspaper columns for the names of servicemen who were missing in action, those who were wounded and those who had perished. Battle casualties were being returned at the rate of 1,200 per day. The number of European civilian fatalities mounted under heavy Allied bombing of

German cities such as Dresden and the continued air assault on Berlin. U.S. Army forces had seized the bridge at Remagen, tightening their grip on the Rhine River. And in the Land of the Rising Sun, much of Tokyo lay in ruins after a B-29 raid under the command of Major General Curtis LeMay. The rain of fire left at least 1,200,000 people homeless.

Even though the United States was spared combat and bombing on the mainland, effects of the war pervaded American society, with almost everyone making some kind of sacrifice to defeat the Axis powers. For too many families, the sacrifice was a loved one. For others, it was having to limit or go without items that were being rationed. For most, it was the sacrifice of their way of life. Before the war, few Arkansans saw uniformed soldiers unless they lived near a base, but after the bombing of Pearl Harbor, military installations served in various capacities throughout the state. Camp Joseph T. Robinson (now simply called Camp Robinson) in Pulaski County was special. With a fluid population of fifty thousand, it was not only a training base for soldiers and medics but also a prisoner-of-war camp and a hospital. The most severely wounded veterans were treated there. Among visitors who hoped to lift the spirits of the patients was Sir Richard Wood, who in March 1945 was on a goodwill tour of the United States with his parents, Lord and Lady Halifax. Lord Halifax was the British ambassador to the United States. Sir Richard shared a special solidarity with the men at whose bedsides he stopped. He himself had suffered grievous injuries in battle, losing both his legs in action in North Africa.

Lord Halifax gave a rousing speech to a conference of city and state luminaries. He paid tribute to the American marines' bravery at the ongoing Battle of Iwo Jima. He also saluted U.S. citizens on the homefront who volunteered their time and energy for civil defense, the Red Cross and other organizations.

At the height of military production, as many as twenty-five thousand people—mostly women—found gainful employment at Arkansas's ordnance plants. Besides the one in Camden, five other munitions facilities were located in the state, and it was in front of the Maumelle Ordnance Plant near the Marche community on US 65 that Red Hall hitched a ride with J.D. Newcomb Jr.

Newcomb was the chief boiler inspector for the State Labor Department and was chairman of the National Board of Boiler and Pressure Vessel Inspectors, where he was known to his many friends as Jimmie. Around noon on Thursday, the eighth of March, he left Little Rock and headed for Clarksville, where he was to make an inspection at a factory. Always willing

Soldiers, trained at Camp Robinson, going off to war. *Arkansas National Guard Archives*.

to lend a helping hand, he didn't think twice about giving a ride to the young man who was thumbing his way northward. And so it was that Newcomb began his short, unexpected journey with the Bringer of Death.

Newcomb's family became worried when he didn't come home Thursday night, and the next morning, the Clarksville factory manager, who had expected Newcomb, called the Labor Department to report he had never reached his destination. A bulletin alerted police to be on the lookout for the missing man's 1941 Oldsmobile. That afternoon, a Cleburne County farm couple, Lois and Elmer Williams, discovered a partially burned car in a glade about two hundred yards from their home. A closer look revealed a charred body inside the vehicle. Aghast at the awful sight, the Williamses hightailed it into Heber Springs to summon officials. The body was on the backseat floorboard, and blood from inside the car had spilled out onto the running board and blown back onto the rear fender in a fine spray that indicated the killer had driven at a fairly high rate of speed. Nightfall prevented further examination of the site, but just after dawn, Sheriff T.L. Turney contacted the state police. Captain Scroggin and Sergeant Sims rushed to assist in the investigation.

A scrap of white cloth with a small blue stripe design was found in the ashes, along with a dozen false teeth from an upper plate. Though the body was burned beyond recognition, Scroggin and Sims thought the victim was probably the missing boiler inspector because the make and model of the car matched Newcomb's. The next day, dental records confirmed the lawmen's suspicions.

Faulkner County sheriff Clarence O. Woodruff expressed his belief that Newcomb had been murdered somewhere around Conway because his route would have taken him there to the US 64/65 split. Instead of turning west toward Clarksville, however, he or the killer proceeded northward. Woodruff also said a waitress in a Conway restaurant had identified a picture of Newcomb as that of a man who had eaten there with a group of other customers around 2:00 p.m. on the day of the murder. Before the sighting was proven erroneous, fear caused some Conway citizens to suspect the killer was still in their midst. A twenty-one-year-old youth on a bicycle found himself in the clutches of Conway police shortly after they received a report that someone had stolen a bike from little Tommy Markham while he was attending a Boy Scout meeting at the Second Baptist Church. Seeing what appeared to be poorly washed-out bloodstains on the man's shirt, city officers notified the ASP, and within forty-five minutes, two state troopers had arrived to take the alleged thief in for questioning. He said he was only en route to visit his mother in Little Rock, and he produced the proper papers to prove he had been in Russellville, registering for the draft.

State and local lawmen asked the public for calm and for any knowledge that might shed light on this most recent murder. It was thought to be connected to the other hitchhike killings, especially since Newcomb had customarily accommodated travelers in need of rides. Like the previous victims, he had been shot with a .38-caliber slug, but this time the bullet wound was to the face, not the back of the head, as if he hadn't gone down without a fight. When members of the National Board of Boiler Inspectors learned about their chairman's tragic death, Secretary C.O. Myers offered a $500 reward for information leading to the capture and conviction of the fiend who had perpetrated the cowardly act. B.T. Harris on behalf of himself and the Arkansas Butane Dealers Association added another $500, and North Little Rock's Elks Lodge No. 1004, to which Newcomb had belonged, pitched in $100.

Two boys, who had been fishing off a bridge over the Little Red River, came forward and said they had seen a man driving an Oldsmobile with a flat tire. He turned off AR 25 onto a logging road and went through a fence.

"He was going pretty fast," one of the boys said. "When he came to a gate in the barb-wire fence, he didn't even slow down. Just drove right through it and into the woods."

A bus driver, in route from Batesville to Little Rock, stated a man in a blue-gray overcoat flagged him down near a suspension bridge at Tumbling Shoals six miles north of Heber Springs about 4:30 p.m. Newcomb was last seen wearing a bluish-gray overcoat with a half-belt in the back.

"Yeah," the driver said. "The coat didn't fit him very well. And I thought it was odd, him being out there, a funny place to catch a bus ride."

"Did he say anything?" Scroggin asked.

"No, he just boarded and took a seat."

"Did you know any of the other passengers? Maybe they can help us."

"Sorry, no, and I didn't notice where that fella got off."

All anyone knew was that the stranger had hopped a bus that was headed back to Little Rock.

"We're probably looking for a local boy," Scroggin said to Sims, as they drove back to headquarters. "Most hitchhikers who make a living by robbing drivers slip in and out of a state before a pattern is noticed, especially if they kill their victims. And they take the vehicles. But this guy, this guy is different. He's sticking around."

"Whoever he is, he's getting sloppy," Sims said. "This kill was a lot messier."

As with the other slayings, robbery was thought to be the motive. Newcomb's watch was missing. It was a white gold Elgin engraved with his monogram JDN. Scroggin said that if the watch had been on the victim when the car was set ablaze, its melted metal would have been found in the ashes. The investigators were still looking for the timepieces stolen from E.C. Adams.

Six days after Newcomb's body was found, Captain Scroggin got an early morning tip from a woman who called and said she had information pertaining to the Hamilton case. Before continuing, she asked for anonymity, and Scroggin gave her his word that her identity would remain confidential. With that promise, she told him she knew an ex-con, Lonnie Blaine, and he was acquainted with a taxi driver named James Hall. On or about the date of Hamilton's slaying, Blaine loaned his car to Hall, who said he had to take care of some business with a bootlegger in Camden. Inside the car's side pocket was a .45-caliber revolver. When Hall returned the car, Blaine checked the gun and discovered two rounds were missing from the chamber. Soon afterward, he heard about Hamilton's murder and that the Camden barber/bootlegger had been shot with a .45. Blaine reached a logical conclusion. He couldn't afford to come clean with the cops, though, for fear of being implicated in the murder himself. He sold the gun and hoped the whole thing would blow over.

Immediately after sending Sims and Oliphant to bring Blaine in for questioning, Scroggin called LRPD detective chief Martin and relayed the news and the name of the suspected hitchhike killer.

"You're joking," Martin could hardly believe it. "We arrested Hall a couple of weeks ago for beating up a guy in a barroom brawl. Not only that, but we questioned him last year in the disappearance of his wife."

It was Scroggin's turn to say, "Now *you're* joking."

"No, siree. We may have just solved the Fay Hall disappearance *and* the hitchhike killings in one fell swoop."

"We're taking care of Blaine. Why don't you do the honors of arresting Hall," Scroggin offered. "We can worry about jurisdiction later."

"I appreciate that," Martin said.

"But before we question Hall, we'll get what we can out of Blaine."

"Do you think he took part in the murders?'

"I doubt it," Scroggin said. "All indications are that this has been a one-man killing spree."

"OK. Well, we'll have that 'one man' in custody by ten o'clock," Martin beamed with satisfaction. His face was redder than usual when he called Peterson and Judd into his office and brought them up to speed.

Judd grinned broadly, and Peterson raised his eyebrows.

"Go see if Mr. Hall can honor us with his presence," Martin joked.

"With pleasure," Peterson said, as he and Judd grabbed their jackets and set out for the taxi stand.

The manager, Fred Vernan, had a good memory for faces and recognized the detectives from their visit several months before.

"We're here to see James Hall again," Peterson said.

"You're in luck. We just hired him back a couple of hours ago. He'd been gone a while, but you remember I told you he just up and quits but comes back again."

"Is he here now?" Peterson asked, looking around.

"No, he's taking a fare to War Memorial Park, but he should be back any minute. Y'all want some coffee while you wait?"

"I wouldn't mind a cup," Judd said, but Peterson declined.

As Vernan poured the brew, Judd expressed condolences for the president of the cab company, who had just died.

"Yeah, Lilbourn was a great boss," Vernan said. "I noticed Chief Martin will be one of the honorary pallbearers."

"Mm-hmm," Judd said. "I think they were pretty good friends."

"He had a lot of friends across the board, everybody from the well-to-do to the shoe-shine boy." Vernan chewed the fat with the detectives in between answering the phone and assigning drivers.

"I sure hope Red's not in trouble with the law," he remarked.

"Is that a fact?" Peterson said.

"Yeah, he knows the city so well, this is a perfect job for him. And he's good-natured and friendly. Oh, there he is." Vernan nodded toward the curb where Hall had just pulled up. Red looked the part of a cabbie with his chauffeur's cap cocked back jauntily on his head. He was counting the cash in his hands, as he walked over to Vernan.

"Got another fare for me?" he asked.

"Well, I did," Vernan said, "But these fellas need to see you about something."

"You remember us? Detectives Peterson and Judd." Peterson flashed his badge.

Without skipping a beat, Red flashed a big smile right back at them.

"Why, sure," he said. "Do you have news about Fay?"

"Not exactly," Judd said. "We just have some questions for you. We'll give you a ride to the station."

"Sure thing," Red sounded as if he were going out for a drink with the boys. "Fred, I'll be back soon." He didn't see the subtle, amused glance exchanged between the two lawmen.

During the ten-minute ride to police headquarters, Red gabbed away. "I guess you heard I got in a little scrape with a guy at a bar."

"Uh-huh," Peterson acknowledged.

"That was just a misunderstanding. Besides, I paid the fine."

"Uh-huh," Peterson repeated himself.

"Well, if this is about Fay, the last I heard she was in California."

The cops didn't say anything, so Red filled the silence with protestations that he was the aggrieved party in the breakup of his marriage.

True to Chief Martin's word, the detectives had Red in custody before 10:00 a.m. At the station, Red submitted to a search of his person and clothing without protest. Lieutenant Oscar F. "Jack" Deubler processed him, taking him to a back room for fingerprinting and mug shots. After putting him in a cell, they went through his possessions and in his billfold found a parcel post receipt that had been mailed from Camden on February 2, the day after Adams's murder. It was addressed to Corinne Franklin, who lived at 412½ Center Street in Little Rock.

Red was unperturbed about the turn of events. He did wonder why they had jailed him without questioning him first, but he was a big fan of detective magazines and knew about various interrogation techniques. Sometimes cops would let a suspect sweat for a while, fret about what clues he might have left behind, all this to throw him off his game and make him panic when they did start grilling him. But Red was confident they would never charge him with Fay's murder. They couldn't prove anything without a body, couldn't even prove she was dead. He smiled to himself, remembering the special place he had chosen for Fay on a humid night in September. He barely gave a thought about the trail of other bodies he had left strewn around Arkansas, but one little nagging doubt wiggled and squirmed in the back of his crafty brain. The day before his arrest, he had left something undone. He had failed to follow his gut instinct. Would that lapse in caution be his downfall?

6

"A NICE, CLEAN BOY"

While Red was cooling his heels in the city jail, Lonnie Blaine was busy answering questions at state police headquarters. He was nervous but cooperative and gave detectives the name of the man who had bought the .45 from him. After retrieving the gun, it took Lieutenant Templeton less than thirty minutes to prove that the bullets from Hamilton's fatal wounds had been fired from Blaine's revolver.

At the same time state law enforcement counterparts were leaning on Blaine, Peterson and Judd went to 1522 Magnolia Street, where Red had been renting a room from Fannie Rose. He had occupied the front bedroom for the last eight weeks, but Rose told the investigators that he was going to move out that very day.

"I asked him to make other arrangements just last night," she said.

> But not because he was a bad tenant. He strikes me as a nice, clean boy. Just the other day he offered to help me with my yard work. He comes into my part of the house and listens to the radio, sometimes for a half hour at a time. He'll listen to the radio and talk to me. He's real friendly. He doesn't smoke or drink or swear, and he always pays his rent on time, even ahead of time. He's paid up 'til Tuesday right now. I used to lock my door at night. But he was so nice I left it unlocked the last week or so.

"If he's such a good boarder, why'd you ask him to move?" Peterson asked. Rose replied,

Well, his constant comings and goings began to worry me. I thought he might be a gambler, although he told me he bought and sold hogs and cattle. Later, I heard him tell somebody on the phone that the government wouldn't let him do that anymore, as only dealers are allowed to do that kind of work. I decided to rent the room to a woman who had asked about it.

"How did he take the news that he had to leave?" Judd asked.

"He was sweet as could be. He said, 'That's all right. I'll probably get another place soon.'"

"He will in a manner of speaking," Peterson said wryly.

"What's all this about?" Rose asked. "Was I right about him being a gambler?"

"I'm sorry, ma'am, but we can't comment on pending charges at this time," Judd replied.

Newspaper headlines would tell her soon enough that she had been sleeping under the same roof with a multiple murderer.

"We need to look around his room," Peterson said, and Rose obliged. She lingered in the doorway while the detectives searched the premises.

A Bible and a detective magazine lay on a table near the bed. The Bible looked as if it had never been read, but the magazine had a corner turned down at a description of how guns could be identified by comparing bullets fired from the weapons. A .32-caliber handgun was lying atop the bureau, and as Peterson went through the dresser drawers, Judd searched the closet, where he found a bluish-gray coat like the one Newcomb had been wearing. Also in the closet was a car cushion, and on close inspection, the detectives found a watch hidden inside the cushion. The initials JDN were engraved on the back of the timepiece. That was an important discovery, as was a box of .38-caliber bullets, but they wanted the .38 revolver itself in order to tie Hall to the Adams and Mulherin murders, as well as Newcomb's.

From Rose's home, Peterson and Judd went to Corinne Franklin's apartment on Center Street and asked her about the parcel post package she had received from Hall. She acknowledged that she was a friend of Hall's, though she denied a relationship of a more intimate nature. She was forthright about the package and produced it for the detectives. It contained a razor, shaving mug, needles and razor blades. They didn't expect to find the traveler's checks or cigarettes—sold or used, they figured.

When asked if there had been anything else in the box, Franklin said, "Yes, there was an electric clock. I bought it from Red for five dollars."

Peterson took possession of the clock, and Judd confiscated the box of other items. Back at headquarters, Judd called Adams's widow and asked her once again to describe the clocks that her husband had carried with him. She gave enough information for Peterson and Judd to conclude that the electric clock had, indeed, belonged to Adams, but the brown alarm clock with the cigarette burn mark on its case wasn't in the box. They decided to go back to Hall's room and search it again. Detective Chief Martin accompanied them. They didn't find the alarm clock, but going through a dresser drawer a second time, they found the .38 Smith & Wesson tucked between some shirts. Martin sent the gun to the ASP, and in no time flat, Lieutenant Templeton matched the gun to the bullets that killed Adams, Mulherin and Newcomb.

It had been a rewarding day for all the lawmen on the case. They went home and had a good night's sleep while Red lay on a cot in jail.

RED WAS LEFT ALONE all day Friday, left alone to contemplate his uncertain future. Detectives thought the strategy would work in their favor when they finally confronted him with all the evidence they had gathered against him. At seven o'clock Friday evening, they transferred him from his city accommodations to state police headquarters, where they had laid several items out on a table and covered them with papers, a staging for what they hoped would be a quick confession. Attending the interrogation were Captain Scroggin, Lieutenants Templeton and Oliphant and Sergeant Sims. LRPD detectives Peterson and Judd were present, and from the *Arkansas Gazette* newspaper was police beat reporter Joe Wirges.

Wirges had a long history and good relationship with lawmen. He was the reporter most respected by police from all agencies: the LRPD, the ASP, the Sheriff's Office—even the two state prison farms, Tucker and Cummins. He was fishing buddies with Lee Henslee, the penitentiary's assistant superintendent. The two would drop their lines in the Arkansas River where it ran behind Cummins. Wirges sometimes spent nights in one of the cells there or on death row at Tucker, where he became a confidant to many of the convicts. He had started out at the *Gazette* as a copy boy in 1913 and then went on to cover the crime beat for forty-nine years until his retirement. He looked the part of a cop—a gruff, no-nonsense kind of guy with a crew cut that accentuated his prominent ears. The police opened up to him and trusted him as if he were one of their own. Sometimes, he helped them type reports. He also had an innate sleuthing ability that came in handy, and he took the pictures that accompanied his articles, once taking particular pride in the photo of a decapitated murder victim. His boss nixed that one, considering it too strong for the stomachs of the morning paper's readers who might be eating breakfast while perusing the news. When Wirges was out in the field, he would call the newsroom and dictate the copy, his deep, gravelly voice easily recognizable. He had a talent for rooting out the odd and unusual, the naturally funny. One time, many years after the Red Hall story, he called the copy room from Cummins Prison and dictated an article to Ernest Dumas, who himself became a revered newsman.

"Hey Ernie," Wirges said, "I've got a great story here. You ready?"

That's how he usually started a dictation. "You ready?"

Dumas put paper in the typewriter, and Wirges began the front-page article.

"A man who had been in Arkansas jails the last four months got a physical examination this morning and turned out to be," Wirges paused for dramatic effect before giving Dumas the kicker, "a woman. Her custodians were confounded. The prisoner is now listed as David Reginald Van Rippy, 29, white female, but she reached the penitentiary two days ago designated as 'white male.' She had pleaded guilty to a charge of bigamy."

After finishing the report, Wirges told Dumas about the reaction from one of Van Rippy's spouses: "I called Van Rippy's wife in Oklahoma, and I said, 'Ma'am, the prison guards took his clothes off to give him a physical...and uh, Mrs. Van Rippy, he's a...turns out...he's a...a woman.' And she said, 'You're kiddin'!' After two or three seconds, she added, 'You know, I always thought there was something different about him.'"

Yes, Wirges was full of such stories—the outrageous, the quirky, the bizarre. What would he make of Red Hall?

When Red was escorted into the interrogation room, he was as relaxed as a snake sunning himself on a rock. Facing the men seated around a table, he joked, "I thought you guys had forgotten me."

"No chance of that," Peterson said, standing up and pulling out a chair. Red sat down, but Peterson stayed on his feet.

"You already know Detective Judd and me," Peterson said. "These other men are with the state police. Captain Scroggin, Sergeant Sims and Lieutenants Templeton and Oliphant." Peterson gestured toward each man, then

Reporter Joe Wirges. *Copyright Arkansas Democrat-Gazette.*

realized he'd left out somebody. "Oh, and this is Joe Wirges. He's practically one of us."

Everybody laughed, including Hall, even though he didn't know why.

"Joe's a reporter for the *Arkansas Gazette*," Oliphant explained. "He's been covering the hitchhike murders. You've read about those, haven't you?"

"I don't read the paper that much," was Red's only comment.

"Would you like a cigarette?" Judd offered.

"No, thanks. I don't smoke. 'The body is the temple of the Holy Spirit,'" Red quoted 1 Corinthians.

"So you wouldn't have any use for cigarettes if you found some?" Sims asked.

"I reckon not," Hall said and then laughed. "Well, maybe if I found some, I could sell them." He glanced casually at the papers on the table in front of him and then said, "Listen, I know you fellers think I killed my wife, but all I know is she left me."

"Why would she leave you?" Peterson asked as he walked to the far end of the table.

"You'd have to ask her that."

"Well, see, that's the problem. She's not here to answer," Peterson approached again. "Why don't you come clean with us?"

"What do you mean?" he asked.

"Tell us what you did to her," Peterson pressed.

"I didn't do anything to her."

Hall's eyes strayed to the papers on the table. When Scroggin shifted in his chair, his hand *accidentally* moved a paper to reveal a clock underneath. Red was puzzled. The clock looked familiar.

"Mrs. Clemmons told us you used to hit Fayrene," Peterson said. "She saw the bruises herself."

Red didn't have time to respond before being confronted about his violent tendencies.

"You like to hit women, don't you?" Peterson said, pacing back and forth, always returning to get down in Red's face.

"No, of course not." Red came to his senses. "Fay and I just tussled. You know how it is between a man and his wife. I told Mrs. Clemmons that. Fay's folks just don't like me."

Peterson backed off, and Judd spoke up.

"Why don't you tell us a little bit about yourself, Red. You don't mind if we call you 'Red'?"

"Everybody does," Hall grinned. "What do you want to know about me? I'm just a working stiff."

"Would you like a cup of coffee?" Judd asked.

"No, that's OK," Red declined.

"It's no trouble."

"No, thanks."

For two hours, Red deflected questions with asides about the adversities he had suffered in life. Almost coming to tears at times, he mentioned his harsh upbringing, the baby he and Walcie had lost at birth and his aborted naval career. At one point he tapped his head and said, "Something seemed to snap up here a long time ago."

"You used to farm, didn't you?" Judd asked. "That's hard work."

"You can say that again," Red agreed. "Yeah, driving a cab's not so bad. Pays pretty good."

"But you take off quite a bit, don't you?" Sims said. "Travel around."

"I guess so. I get restless." He paused. "But they always hire me back. That ought to tell you something."

"What does that tell us?" Peterson asked.

Red looked at Peterson for several seconds. "Well, they like me there at the cab company. They know they can trust me."

Peterson snickered and turned his back to Hall. Red straightened up in his chair.

"Been out of town lately?" Oliphant asked, and Scroggin moved another paper on the table, revealing the .32 pistol.

Red was rattled. Noticeably so. After a gap of silence, he answered, "Yeah." He drew the word out, making it sound like two syllables.

"Where'd you go?" Sims asked.

"No place special."

As the questioning continued, Red's emotions seesawed back and forth. Peterson sat down occasionally but sprang up quickly when he sensed a weakening in Hall's resolve. Bouncing back and forth from queries about Fayrene's disappearance to the hitchhike murders knocked Red off balance a time or two. The grilling was taking its toll.

"Tell us more about yourself," Judd said. "You have a son, don't you?"

The tension in Red's body left him, and he smiled proudly. "I do. My first wife and I have a little boy. I'm crazy about him."

"Then why don't you do the right thing by him?" Peterson put his fists on his hips, and the flare of his jacket exposed his holstered gun.

"I don't know what you're getting at," Red steadfastly played the innocent, but Peterson sensed he had hit a nerve.

"Do you want that little boy to be like you when he grows up? Wandering around, never having a normal home life. What kind of father are you?"

"I provide for him," Hall said.

"He needs more from you than a few dollars a month. He needs to know that his daddy didn't try to squirm out of taking responsibility for what you've done. Do you want him to remember you as a coward?"

Red's bravado withered.

With one hand on the table and the other on the back of Hall's chair, Peterson urged him to confess, "Be a man and take the consequences."

At that moment, Scroggin uncovered the .38 revolver. Hall blanched and then threw his hands out in a gesture of compliance. Tipping his chair on its back legs, he said, "OK. I'll tell you all about it. I killed 'em all."

7

TRUE CONFESSIONS

Red Hall may not have knocked World War II off the front page of the *Arkansas Gazette*, but the two-column, two-page spread about his crimes and confession certainly gave readers a new topic to discuss. His statements cleared up the four hitchhike murders and his wife's disappearance. Fay, as her family had feared, was dead. Hall also admitted to killing an unidentified Black woman in Salina, Kansas, in 1938. His recitation of his own hard life evoked little sympathy from the public, but that didn't stop him from trying to curry compassion.

"To begin with," he said, "my early life was far from happy. I have nine brothers and sisters living. Another brother died. We had only the bare necessities of life. My father was very strict.

"I married a country girl, but we were divorced after four years. We have a two-year-old boy. I'm crazy about him.

"I married Fay Clemmons of Lonoke on the twenty-second of March last year. She was nineteen. I was crazy about her, but we soon began having trouble. I was driving a cab and making from twenty to fifty dollars a night. She was wasting our money, and this caused many arguments.

"I believe it was last September when I decided I'd had enough of it, so I took her out the Old River Road near the Riverside Golf Course, led her off into a ravine on the river bank and beat her to death with my hands."

At this point in his confession, Hall simulated his murderous actions, using Sergeant Sims as Fay's stand-in.

"I must have hit her more than twenty times over the head. I didn't cover her or make any effort to hide her body. Then I came back to town."

"Will you help us find her body?" Peterson asked.

"Sure," he said. "It won't bother me a bit."

"Tell us about Carl Hamilton," Scroggin prodded him.

"I had gone there planning to commit a robbery, and I met the darky and got him out of town under the pretext of selling him some whiskey. I had Lonnie's .45 revolver. When I tried to rob Hamilton, he drew a .38, so I shot him twice. I took his money, his revolver, and some extra cartridges that I found in his pocket. I used the .38 to kill Mr. Adams, Mr. Mulherin and Mr. Newcomb."

"Hamilton still had a little cash on him," Sims said. "And a knife and ring. Why did you leave those?"

"And a watch," Hall added. "Yeah, well, I thought I heard somebody coming up, so I got out of there."

Red then proceeded to relate how he had killed E.C. Adams.

"I flagged him down on the Arch Street viaduct near Thirty-Third Street and rode almost to Fordyce with him before I drew my revolver and forced him to stop the car. I marched him off the highway about thirty yards and shot him in the head. I got twenty-six dollars from his pockets. I took his two watches and suitcase and even took off his shoes in hunting for money. I took the suitcase to Camden. On the way, I threw away an engraved watch; I sold the other one to a pawnbroker in Alexandria, Louisiana. The suitcase was filled with cigarettes, and I sold them."

Hall admitted selling the electric clock to Corinne Franklin and the brown alarm clock to a stranger who stopped him near Sixth and Center Streets in Little Rock and offered him two dollars for it.

"About a week later," Hall continued, "I hitchhiked to Humnoke where Mr. Mulherin gave me a lift. Near Stuttgart, I pulled my gun and forced him to stop the truck. We got out, walked away to where I didn't think anybody could see us, and then I shot him in the back of the head. He had three or four billfolds and a purse. I got a little more than a hundred dollars from him. There were several checks in the purse, but I threw them and the billfolds and pocketbooks into a ditch full of water. I drove the truck through Stuttgart and left it near the railroad tracks and then I hitchhiked back home with two drivers. The first one took me to Highway 70 and the second into Little Rock."

Hall went on to describe the murder of Newcomb: "I rode a bus from Markham and Main Street to Levy. I remember telling a friend I was going out on the highway to make some money. I thumbed my way to Marche where Mr. Newcomb gave me a ride. About a mile south of Conway, I drew my revolver and forced him to stop his car. He jumped out, but I caught his coattail, and after a short struggle, I pushed him into the backseat. He still showed fight, so I shot him. He must have been looking at me 'cause I think the bullet hit him in the face. He crumpled down on the floorboard and was quiet.

"Funny thing," Hall said, perplexed. "While we were struggling, somebody who was driving by slowed down and almost stopped, but they didn't. Lucky for them." He chuckled. "I drove through Conway and followed Highway 65 North, looking for a river. I had decided to throw the body into a stream but didn't find one large enough to suit me."

In 1945, the Arkansas River was only five miles west of the Conway city limits, and Hall would have known that, so why he didn't dump Newcomb there is a conundrum.

"I kept going until I passed Heber Springs where a rear tire blew out. Then I drove through a wire fence into the woods where I robbed him of about seventy dollars and his watch and coat. I struck a match and lit some papers in the car and left."

When Detective Peterson asked Hall if he had killed any other people, he answered, "No," but quickly corrected himself by saying, "I killed a colored woman in Salina, Kansas, when I was seventeen. I was coming back from a date when she stopped me and asked for change for a dollar. She drew a knife and tried to rob me. I beat her to death. That was on North Santa Fe Street."

At the request of investigators, the *Arkansas Gazette* appealed to the public in recovering E.C. Adams's brown alarm clock and Doyle Mulherin's billfolds. The newspaper promised more articles about the sensational murders, including a first-person account of a trip to be made by law officials and Hall to find Fay Hall's remains.

Scroggin publicly thanked city detectives for their assistance in solving the hitchhike killings, and Martin heaped praise upon his own men, with Peterson receiving special credit for eliciting the confession.

Martin said, "Their efforts were the best piece of detective work turned in here in many years. The whole state should be grateful for their magnificent work."

Scroggin also lauded the performance of his men, Lieutenant Rhett Oliphant and Sergeant Homer Sims.

"These two officers devoted their entire time to the hitchhike cases," Scroggin said.

*They spent the last two months traveling many miles and spending
sleepless nights in efforts to find the slayer. Much of it was tiring, routine
investigation, but they did their job well. The public will never know the
many little things they had to investigate, all of which required much time
and long hours. Their devotion to duty paved the way for the close-in by
Detectives Peterson and Judd. The value of such a department as ours
was clearly demonstrated in this case. It reveals what can be accomplished
with the perfect cooperation between our group and the Little Rock Police
Department. Detectives Peterson and Judd are very competent men, and
when I called on them through Chief of Detectives Martin, I knew the
matter would be given their usual thorough attention. The entire State Police
personnel is proud of removing Hall from the public. He was a menace to
society. Everyone in the state should feel safer with the knowledge that this
callous killer is behind bars.*

Answering congratulatory phone calls from other law enforcement
officers and from community leaders kept Chief Martin busy all day. W.P.
Hamilton of the Houck Music Company gave Martin twenty-five dollars to
be divided between the officers who solved the murders.

"Citizens of the state owe these men plenty," Hamilton said. "It wasn't
safe to be on the highway with such a man at large. I hope a hundred more
men will reward these officers for their great service to the state."

Sheriff Turney conferred with Captain Scroggin about the possible
disbursement of the other $1,100 that had been offered for the arrest and
conviction of J.D. Newcomb's murderer. It was Scroggin's opinion that the
reward should go to the woman who called in the tip that broke the case.
Her identity remained confidential.

On Saturday afternoon, the seventeenth of March, a caravan of lawmen
and reporters left city hall with Red, who gave directions to the place where
he had killed Fay. Still dressed in his taxi driver uniform and cabbie's cap, he
sat handcuffed to Peterson in the back seat of the lead car; Joe Wirges was
to his left. The string of other automobiles paraded to the site off the Old
River Road near the Riverside Golf Course. The trip had been delayed for
several hours due to heavy rains; however, the bad weather lifted at about
3:15 p.m., and it was decided to carry on with the search.

During the ride, as they neared their destination, Wirges asked Hall, "Did
your wife suspect anything when you brought her out here?"

"I don't suppose she did," Red replied.

"Did you feel bad about killing her?"

Detective Herbert Peterson (*left*) and James Waybern "Red" Hall. *Copyright Arkansas Democrat-Gazette.*

"No, my conscience never bothered me."

Also making the journey to the scene of the crime were Captain Scroggin, Sheriff Caple, Prosecuting Attorney Sam Robinson, LRPD patrolman O.A. Allen, two deputies and Detectives Judd, Sims, Oliphant and Templeton. Representing the press, besides Joe Wirges, were Agnes Watson from Little Rock's evening newspaper, the *Arkansas Democrat*, and Dick Allen, a correspondent for the *Memphis Commercial Appeal.*

Red thought he could lead them right to the place in a gulley near the riverbank, so the party parked their cars near the road and walked through woods toward the river several hundred yards away. Once there, however, Hall had a difficult time finding any of his wife's remains.

"I haven't been back here since I killed her, and everything looks different," he explained. "There was a great deal of green leaves on the underbrush then, and now the trees are bare."

The group milled around for about an hour and a half. Peterson, wearing a pin-striped suit, was nursing a head cold and kept a small ten-cent tin of aspirin in his coat pocket. He had removed the handcuffs so Red could poke around in the debris that had piled up as a result of river overflows. Occasionally, the prisoner would stop and look closely at a log or a piece of driftwood.

"I left her uncovered," he said with detachment. "I figured vultures, cats, other animals and water from the river would devour the body."

Just when it seemed as if the searchers would have no luck before sunset, unexpected help arrived in the form of Cecil Foster, a woodcutter who lived across a pasture from the river. While fanning out in a broader search area, Judd and Sims met Foster, who had come down to see what was going on. When he learned the purpose of the gathering, he said, "I may have something that will interest you."

Foster went on to tell the group, "I found part of a skull in the woods here about three months ago, and I took it home. It's there now. I was hauling wood when I saw the skull at the side of the road. I thought it had just washed downriver."

Though everyone else considered it odd that Foster hadn't reported his find to authorities, they were nevertheless grateful for his assistance.

"Sometime later," Foster said, "When I was going for more wood, I saw something I thought was a jawbone, but I didn't stop to pick it up. It was close to a big cottonwood log. Now, let me see." As he looked around, Foster rubbed the stubble on his chin. "Over here, I think."

Prosecuting Attorney Sam Robinson holds Fayrene's skull after Hall (*in cabbie's cap*) led lawmen and reporters to her remains. Also pictured are (*left to right*) reporter Dick Allen, Detective Herbert Peterson, Hall, Lieutenant Rhett Oliphant, unidentified boy and reporter Agnes Watson. *Copyright Arkansas Democrat-Gazette.*

After taking a few long strides, no more than twenty yards away from a spot where Red had searched, Foster found the log.

"Sure 'nough, this is it," he said. "Look in that washed-out holler over there."

Patrolman Allen saw where Foster was pointing and pulled the jawbone out of its hiding place under a stump that had been rolled into the ravine by woodcutters working in the area. A few teeth were still imbedded in the stump.

"That's Fay's alright," Hall said. "See that buck tooth? It used to hurt me when we kissed."

Over the next half hour, the men found other scattered skeletal parts, including ribs, a thigh bone and a shin bone. Detective Judd retrieved a thatch of brown hair about ten feet north of the stump. Sergeant Sims located what was left of a red dress. Scroggin uncovered the shoes that had caused Fay such discomfort at the Rainbow Garden, but no one found a trace of her pocketbook or engagement and wedding rings. Red denied taking the items but said the purse had contained about fifty dollars and the rings were set with rubies and diamonds. He mentioned he had paid fifty dollars for the jewelry when he and Fay were married.

"You know what?" he said, amused by a sudden realization. "Our first anniversary would've been less than a week from now."

THE CLEMMONS FAMILY HAD been notified of the intended search beforehand and had left their farm and gone to Little Rock to await the outcome. When Ada learned of her daughter's fate, she said, "Red will have only a moment's pain when he dies for this, but no one knows how long my girl suffered before she died."

The family expressed regret that Hall hadn't been apprehended before the subsequent murders.

"We went to the detectives several times after Fay disappeared and asked them to take action," her father told reporters, "But we realized they couldn't without any proof. The police did all they could."

Clemmons asked Martin if he could talk with Hall for a few minutes.

"I wouldn't harm him in the least," Clemmons promised.

> I don't want personal vengeance. I feel the courts will mete out the proper punishment to him. Let the law take care of that for us. But that won't bring Fay back. I would just like to see Red and talk to him. I don't want to touch him. I have no ill-feeling toward any member of his family. I have a few things to ask him, things that could ease our worries.

Martin said he thought the meeting could be arranged and advised Clemmons to speak with Prosecuting Attorney Robinson. Clemmons left instructions for authorities to contact a Lonoke funeral home about when Fay's remains would be released. "Her mother and I plan to bury her back home," he said.

When detectives learned that Hall had driven his car to California after killing his wife and then hitchhiked back, they realized he might have murdered other people during the trip and all of his other journeys. His picture and fingerprints were distributed to police departments across the country, and as word spread about the hitchhike killer, calls came in from law enforcement agencies in several states, including Oklahoma, Kansas, California, Oregon, New Mexico, Texas, Louisiana and New York. Officers in Topeka, Kansas, wanted to ask Hall whether he had any connection to the Lambert/Nipper slayings near Canton, Kansas.

In response to the appeal to the public for information about the items that Hall had stolen from his victims, William J. Baker said he had bought an alarm clock from a man on the street. Though he correctly stated that the price had been two dollars, the description he gave didn't jive with that of E.C. Adams's clock. Then detectives heard from Seaman First Class John McGlothan, who gave them a clock that he had bought from a stranger near Sixth and Louisiana Streets about a month before. It did match the description: it had a brown case with a cigarette burn and Adams's name was scratched in paint on the case, leaving no doubt about its authenticity. McGlothan made a positive identification of Hall as the man who had sold the clock to him.

The Red Hall story made minor celebrities out of ordinary citizens who had crossed his path and lived to tell the tale. It was a hot newspaper story, and readers couldn't get enough of it. Reporters were eager to get quotes.

The landlady Fannie Rose said: "It makes me lose my breath when I think of it. I feel terrible inside. The idea of him going out and killing those people and then crawling back into bed in my house!" The paper described the premises and Rose thusly: "The mild-mannered Grandmother Rose lived alone with the killer in her clean, well-furnished, stone bungalow."

Red's co-workers were just as shocked. A sampling of their reactions to the news that he was a cold-blooded killer: "He was a swell guy." "Willing to help anyone." "Nearly always smiling."

Former schoolmates didn't share such fond remembrances of Red. Some said he was a "tough boy" who carried a blackjack and was often spoiling for a fight.

A man named Albert Johnson of North Little Rock also remembered Red Hall. He contacted police and said he recognized Hall's newspaper picture as that of a man he had picked up at the intersection of AR 11 and US 70 about 3:00 p.m. on the day of the Mulherin murder.

"That fellow sure was nervous," Johnson said of Hall.

I became alarmed and watched him continuously. I decided to hit him if he put his hands in his pockets. He kept looking back and couldn't sit still. I bought three packages of cigarettes from him for sixty cents. He told me he didn't smoke. I became so alarmed that I stopped at the County Merchant's Store a few miles from Little Rock, pretending I had a headache and needed to rest. He boarded a bus, and I went home. I believe he intended to rob me but there was probably too much traffic on the highway.

Hall admitted that he and Johnson's hitchhiker were one and the same. Would he have robbed Johnson? "The thought crossed my mind," he said.

After helping authorities find his wife's skeletal remains on that dreary Saturday outing, Red got a good night's sleep and then spent the Sabbath in calm reflection. Detective Chief Martin granted him two requests. Red wanted the twenty-four dollars that he was carrying when arrested so he could buy some fruit, and he also asked for a Bible.

"I want to prepare myself to go to Heaven," he said. "I've been baptized in the Baptist church and have read the Bible a long time. I know what it is, and I feel certain of my salvation. I'm not worried on that score. The only thing that bothers me is this confinement. I don't like to be cooped up. The world would be better off without me."

On Monday, a well-rested and accommodating Red Hall agreed to take a trip to Stuttgart with the police. Homer Sims sat in the front seat of the first car with Patrolman Allen, who was driving. Wirges sat in back with Red, who was once again handcuffed to Detective Peterson. As before, several other cars carried reporters and more lawmen, including Oliphant and Judd. Hall started giving a play-by-play commentary of Doyle Mulherin's last minutes on Earth.

"This is where he picked me up," Hall said, pointing out the spot in Lonoke County. "But I didn't pull my gun right then."

As the detail of cops and prisoner drove on, Red analyzed the methods of several hitchhikers they passed on the road. Many, he predicted, would end up walking most of the way. He then explained his own technique in the fine art of getting a free ride.

"I betcha I could get out on the highway right now and get a ride with the first or second driver who came along. It's not the way you wiggle your thumb or the gesture you make," he instructed. "It's all in the look you give the driver. It's the same about anything else. I could walk up to a perfect stranger and ask him for twenty dollars. I wouldn't have to ask many before I'd get it."

The car clattered over a wooden bridge that spanned a stream flowing along part of the western border of the Arkansas Grand Prairie.

"This is where I forced Mr. Mulherin to pull over," Hall said after they crossed into Prairie County.

They stopped and got out of the car, but Red couldn't find the exact spot where he killed Mulherin. The water level in the ditches was much higher than it had been the previous month. Recent rains had left some of the gravel road under swirling water. As it so happened, March 1945 was an unusually wet month. Flooding across the entire state threatened railroad bridges and forced the closure of busy highways. The hardpan of the Arkansas Grand Prairie doesn't let rainwater seep deep into the ground. The subsoil is hard clay, not conducive to many crops but an excellent venue for rice, so fields stay wet throughout the growing season. The ever-present water in the rice fields attracts ducks, and that's how, in the 1930s, the title of the Rice and Duck Capital of the World was claimed by the Arkansas town with a German name.

"We'll be in Stuttgart soon," Allen said, as the men climbed back into the car and continued on their way.

The dark clouds on the horizon and the cool, damp air seemed more like harbingers of autumn than the welcome mat for spring. The Arkansas Grand Prairie, like the Western Plains, allowed an unobstructed view of faraway traffic. Ordinarily, such a wide expanse of divinely open space would have lifted Red out of the doldrums with reminisces of his vagabond days, but the presence of his captors and the gloom surrounding them reminded him of his stark county lodgings to which he would soon return. Oh, how he hated the gray tightness of a jail cell.

Nearing town, Allen asked, "Anybody hungry?"

Red snapped out of his sorrowful abyss and realized his stomach did feel empty.

"I could go for a hamburger," he said.

Sergeant Sims seconded the notion, adding, "I hear meat rations are about to drop again."

"12 percent," Wirges said, "The lowest since the Depression, but times are tough all over. Did you read about Germany making farmers in the Reich plant potatoes instead of tobacco?"

"I'm glad we have you to edify us, Joe," Peterson teased. "I can live without potatoes, but cigars? I don't know about that."

"Cigars?" Wirges expressed surprise. "You must make more money than I thought."

"I seem to recall you smoking a stogie now and then."

"Only when I want to impress somebody."

Road sign showing speed limit during World War II. *Library of Congress.*

Hall was still somewhat drowsy with daydreams of freedom, but he noticed that Allen didn't come to a complete stop at an intersection.

"I went to the right," he said, recalling the route he had taken after shooting Mulherin. "And I stopped for that stop sign. That's one thing I never did. I never violated the law."

The officers laughed.

"I mean traffic laws," Red amended his claim sheepishly. Suggesting a café on Maple Street, he said, "I left Mulherin's truck near the railroad tracks there."

After grabbing a bite to eat, the officers followed Red's directions to Maple and Second. There he pointed to a storm sewer where he had thrown the keys to Mulherin's vehicle. While Hall and Peterson stood by, the other men tried to find the keys but were unsuccessful. They called in the Stuttgart Fire Department to pump the basin dry, only to learn that the basin had been cleaned the preceding day. Street workers who had done the cleaning led the officers to the city dump, but searching through the heaps of garbage was deemed hopeless and impractical, so Red took the next step.

"There's a bigger storm sewer in the 400 block of Main Street," he said. "That's where I threw the pocketbooks."

But even with volunteers helping them search, the officers couldn't find the discarded evidence. They decided to call it a day. On their way back to Little Rock, Red mused aloud about a mistake that had tripped him up.

"My guilt wouldn't have been proved if I had followed my instinct the day before they arrested me. I was going to get rid of the .38," Hall said, referencing the revolver that he had used in three murders. "I had it hidden in my room, and I thought the officers never would find it. You know that .32-caliber pistol I left on my dresser?"

Peterson and Wirges nodded affirmatively.

"I thought if the officers ever searched the room, they would be content with that one weapon. I knew it couldn't be connected to any of the killings."

"We overlooked the .38 at first," Peterson told him.

"That's just what I thought you'd do," Red laughed with satisfaction.

"It was your supply of .38-caliber ammunition that kept them looking for the gun," Wirges said. "They found it between some shirts in the dresser drawer."

"But the parcel post receipt was the first piece of material evidence that tied you to the Adams murder," Peterson told him.

"Where was it?" Hall had to be reminded.

"In your billfold."

"Did I leave that thing in there?" He was genuinely surprised by his own error. "In the first place it was worthless, and there was no reason for me to keep it. That sure was a bad mistake." He shook his head and for a few moments looked downright depressed.

The following day, again accompanied by officers and reporters, Hall retraced the route he had taken with the body of J.D. Newcomb Jr. Halfway between Little Rock and Conway, at the geographic center of Arkansas, floodwaters caused a delay, slowing traffic to a crawl. Workmen were fighting to save the Missouri Pacific Railroad track at Palarm Creek. They were moving the track and trestle several feet to the east where filler had been hauled in, making a new roadbed. The flooding had swept nine coal cars and boxcars into the river before cresting. A couple of the cars were still visible.

As the procession passed through Conway, Faulkner County sheriff Clarence O. Woodruff joined it. Hall reiterated his intent to dispose of the dead man in a body of water, but for some hard-to-fathom reason, he kept driving past areas that had access to the Arkansas River, the Little Red River and various streams. All the while, Newcomb's blood was visible on the car's exterior. The trip covered 238 miles one way. From Conway, he had followed US 65 to Clinton, where he turned onto AR 9. About four miles later, he asked the driver to pull over near a shallow stream called Pee Dee Creek.

"I stopped here," he said. "And went through Mr. Newcomb's pockets."

"Was it worth it?" Peterson asked, trying to picture Hall greedily robbing the corpse.

"The way I was thinking at the time, it was."

They continued on toward the small town of Shirley, crossing the Middle Fork of the Little Red River along the way.

"I thought about throwing Mr. Newcomb in the water here," Hall said, "But I nixed that idea on account of being too close to town."

The hamlet consisted primarily of a garage, post office, general store and gas station, all on the four corners of a crossroads. Again, the officers were amazed by Hall's confusing thought processes as he continued to direct the itinerary.

"I turned around and went south back to Clinton and then changed my mind and headed northeast again," he said.

Around noon they stopped for lunch in Mountain View, a little town that hadn't seen so much excitement since former resident Dick Powell had hit it big in Hollywood. Word about the group's trip spread fast throughout other communities in the area. As they sat down to eat, Peterson removed the prisoner's handcuffs so Hall wouldn't be as readily identified by the curiosity-seekers who began to stream into the cafe. A short time later, an old man came up to where Peterson, Hall and Sims were seated. He asked which one was the notorious killer, and Sims pointed across the room to Joe Wirges, who was sitting at a table with other officers.

"He's over there," Sims said.

The elderly gent peered at Wirges and remarked, "He shore is an ornery-lookin' son-of-a-bitch, ain't he?"

Peterson and Sims kept straight faces, but Red almost choked on his iced tea. For a man who would be facing the death penalty, he sure was having a lot of fun. The motorcade resumed and headed for Independence County.

"This is where I decided to go back to Little Rock," Hall said at the junction of AR 14 and AR 25. "I was going to pitch him in the Arkansas River."

So the group turned around, and just before they reached Mountain View again, Hall told them, "I got off the main road, but you probably shouldn't. I drowned out my car motor when I tried to ford a little stream up there. Had to wait at least fifteen minutes for it to dry."

Crossing the suspension bridge at Tumbling Shoals, Hall said, "My tire blew out here, but I had to go on a couple of miles before I found a side road."

So because of a bad tire, Newcomb's final resting place didn't turn out to be a watery grave.

"I drove as fast as I could before anybody had a chance to see me," Hall said. "But they did, didn't they?"

Oliphant nodded. "Some boys who were out fishing. And the bus driver remembered the coat you were wearing. We figured it was Newcomb's."

"I guess everybody will remember me now," Hall said, enjoying the stardom that he had gained. When they stopped at the courthouse in Heber Springs, his fame drew a throng of about five hundred people. One man in the crowd waved a noose, but he was chased off by Sheriff Turney. Here, handcuffed to Lieutenant Oliphant, Hall was in a genial frame of mind as he looked out over the gathering and was pleased at the big turnout. He smiled broadly and asked that the window be raised so he could converse with the curious. He identified several girls as "old friends" and thought he recognized a man as a distant relative but learned he was mistaken. Another man asked the name of his mother.

"Eva Ingram," Hall replied.

"I know her," the man said.

The crowd reminded Hall of a carnival, and he was the sideshow attraction.

"I could make plenty of money selling peanuts and popcorn," he said.

The Cleburne County Court House in Heber Springs. *Courtesy Cleburne County Historical Society.*

On the way back to Little Rock, the officers stopped in Conway to drop off Sheriff Woodward. While there, they had coffee at the American Grill, and Hall ate again. His guards marveled at his hearty appetite, a testament to his clear conscience.

It has become evident from this chronicle so far that authorities conducted a thorough investigation, what with all the trips. They were still gathering evidence from each crime in order to help determine where Hall's trial would be held. Woodruff thought he should be tried in Faulkner County because of the overwhelming evidence of his guilt in the Newcomb murder, which he committed just outside Conway. But others thought too many of his friends and relatives lived in the area, and bias might play a part in a trial if it were held there.

Hall had become quite comfortable with the lawmen and really connected with Joe Wirges. The reporter had talked about his camaraderie with inmates at the penal farm. Hall began to trust his "entourage" enough to tell them more about his sordid past. It was probably fortunate for the United States that he flunked out of the navy. His loose lips could have sunk a fleet of ships. During a trip to Louisiana and back, he produced the most shocking narrative of his escapades and their horrifying conclusions.

8

"THE PEAK OF PERFECTION"

To bolster the case against Hall and to corroborate his confessions even further, another road trip was made to Alexandria, Louisiana, to retrieve some of the items he had stolen from his victims. The contingent accompanying Hall consisted of Oliphant, Sims, Judd, Peterson and Wirges. On the way to Louisiana, they stopped near Fordyce, where Hall reenacted the killing of E.C. Adams. He remembered tearing the man's shoelaces when he looked for money in the shoes. Afterward, he put all of his ill-gotten gains in Adams's suitcase and hitched a ride into Camden. He surprised everyone when he told them that the man who picked him up was a government official, a Perry County Farm Services agent who was on his way to visit relatives in south Arkansas. The cadre of cops and Hall stopped in Camden briefly so he could point out the pool hall where he had left the rifled suitcase. Then the group continued to Alexandria. There, he led the officers to a jewelry store where he had sold an unusual ring and Adams's watch. The ring was a heavy piece of jewelry with a snake and Hindu design set with a red stone. The store proprietor, C.W. Ingraham, identified Hall as the man who had sold a watch and that ring.

"He wanted to pawn the articles," Ingraham said. "But since we're not licensed to operate a pawn shop, we declined. Then he gave me the most pitiful and convincing story I've ever heard. He gave me his name as H. L. Willis of Bunkie, Louisiana and said he needed money for his buddy who had been arrested for running a red light. I agreed to buy the watch and ring for twenty-five dollars—more than the items were worth—with the understanding he would buy them back Monday morning, but he never returned."

Ingraham told Alexandria chief of police George Gray that the watch had been loaned to a customer who was having his own watch repaired. It was to be sent to Little Rock later.

The ring was a mystery. It wasn't Adams's. Hall said he had bought the ring in Little Rock, but he had no proof and no one believed him. It had been a long week, and everyone was tired, but as the crew headed for home, Hall perked them up with a short statement that astounded them.

"There were others," he said.

"Others?" Peterson raised an eyebrow.

"I've killed other people besides Fay and the four in Arkansas this year. A dozen come to mind right now. That colored woman in Salina, a man in Texas last December, and ten Mexicans in Arizona in 1938. There were more."

"How many are we talking about?" Peterson asked.

"Hmm, nearer twenty-four than twelve," Red estimated.

Nearer twenty-four than twelve. One for each year of his own life, just like Billy the Kid. The killings he claimed as his own doing amounted to seventeen, leaving seven unknown. Possibly more. Though authorities didn't have names for the other victims, they certainly had some good prospects.

Red went on, "The truth is that if I told you about every person I have killed, people wouldn't believe it. There are so many, I can't remember."

When detectives returned Hall to police headquarters, Lieutenant Deubler took more fingerprints. The first batch dwindled fast when officers from other states began making inquiries, hoping to close the books on unsolved murders in their jurisdictions.

On Thursday, Red was moved to city hall, where Oklahoma lawmen questioned him about similar killings in their state. Seminole police chief Jake Sims expressed his belief that Hall was the likely killer of Jim Owen, the chief warehouseman for the Cities Service Oil Company, murdered on December 23, 1940.

"He hasn't admitted anything yet," Sims said, "But he has told us enough about it to convince us that he probably was the one. He said he had been over to Seminole several times, and I remember seeing him there myself."

Captain Floyd Parks with the Oklahoma State Highway Patrol Identification Bureau and Ottawa County sheriff Dee Watters called the LRPD and asked for Hall's fingerprints and photograph, saying that four murders of a comparable type had been committed in the area around Miami, Oklahoma, in the past few months. Parks and Watters then drove to Little Rock, seeking answers that related particularly to the slaying of Wehman Peacock Jr. the previous autumn, but Hall was mum on the subject.

Sheriff Bob Reeves of Franklin, Texas, telegraphed Sheriff Caple asking him to question Hall about the unsolved murder of a man named William Wilcox at Calvert, Texas, on February 1, 1941. The thirty-year-old Wilcox was found beaten to death and robbed in his small grocery store. Reeves said an undetermined amount of money and the victim's watch had been taken. They had no clues about the identity of the assailant. Wilcox lived alone in the back of the store. Caple asked Hall, but Red denied any knowledge of that crime and said he had never been in Calvert.

Captain Manuel T. Gonzaullas with the Texas Rangers sent a member of his force to question Hall about six unsolved slayings that had occurred in 1938. Gonzaullas, nicknamed "Lone Wolf" Gonzaullas, was a favorite among newsmen and photographers because of his flamboyant and charismatic presence. He was often pictured wearing pearl-handled gold-and-silver-plated pistols and riding a white Arabian horse with silver-trimmed bridle and saddle. One case Gonzaullas sought to close was the double homicide of the wealthy Hazel Frome and her adult daughter, Nancy, which occurred near Van Horn, Texas. The women had been beaten, choked, burned and then shot. Those slayings have been attributed to everyone from drug smugglers to Nazi spies. But victims in the other cases mentioned by Gonzaullas were two couples found killed in New Mexico. Hall pleaded ignorance when answering queries by the Rangers.

Remembering the report of Hall being seen in a maroon car with a Texas plate, Chief Martin asked him about the back seat full of Bibles. Hall said he had tried to sell them for a publishing company in Dallas but didn't have much luck, so he quit. He provided his employer's name, and Martin was inclined to believe him. Just in case, though, Martin phoned Dallas chief of detectives J.W. Fritz and asked him to investigate whether a Bible salesman had been reported missing or killed in Texas in late 1944. Fritz said he would look into it.

"I might as well set the record straight about Fayrene, too," Hall told the Arkansas authorities.

She knew too much. She was the most bull-headed woman I ever saw, always wanting to go with me when I traveled. I let her come along when I went to Oregon. I couldn't take a chance she'd talk. But the night I killed her, she went with me willingly to the riverbank. I always seemed to have a knack for gaining the confidence of anyone. Anything I suggested rarely

*brought an argument. I don't know what it is or how to explain it exactly.
This knack helped me get rides on highways with motorists who had passed
up other hitchhikers.*

Arkansas investigators asked him about two unsolved murders that
occurred in Searcy and Pulaski Counties in 1944. A skeleton had been found
near Leslie, and another was discovered on the Twelfth Street Pike in Little
Rock. Hall denied knowledge of either case and also refuted accusations that
he had killed a man near Kerr, Arkansas, in 1942. He did tell Caple he had a
good prospective victim in Little Rock "last year but decided it best not to kill
and rob him." Hall felt sure the crime would have been solved. He identified
the man as a café operator who always carried between $5,000 and $6,000
in his pockets.

"What about your own brother George?" Sheriff Caple asked.

"Gilmer? What about him?" Red responded.

"Did you have anything to do with his disappearance?"

"He left home, and I suppose someone murdered him."

Despite Hall's devil-may-care attitude toward killing people, Caple said
he found Hall to be a "pleasant conversationalist."

After meeting with the out-of-state lawmen, Red left City Hall,
accompanied by Peterson, Judd, Martin, and Wirges. When they got back to
the county jail, Hall's father and a family friend met them on the sidewalk.
Samuel Hall threw his arms around his son. For the first time since the arrest,
Red's nerves broke, and he sobbed. Samuel retained his composure. It was
the first time they had seen each other since Red's capture. They had a short
visit spent mostly in prayer.

Lawmen had, at first, deemed it advisable to suppress the news of other
possible slayings until investigations could be made. They reasoned Hall
might purposely tell of a long list of bloody murders in order to cause a
delay in his trial and also to get special privileges and trips to purported
crime scenes with many stops at restaurants along the way. But word got out,
and Detective Chief Martin made a statement to the press.

He branded Hall

*the most unfeeling, heartless and inhumane killer I've ever known. In all
my twenty-seven years on the detective force, I have never met a man like
him. He talks about murder as if it was commonplace. I do believe he has
committed similar crimes across the nation. He told me he has hitchhiked
over the country since he was fourteen and has visited all except a few of*

the Eastern states. You can't make me believe these slayings he admitted to are his only crimes. We may never be able to connect him to others, but I always will believe he had enough experience in killing that he had about reached the peak of perfection.

Joe Wirges arranged for an exclusive jailhouse interview with Hall, and Red greeted the reporter cordially. He started by explaining the emotional scene that had just occurred with his father.

"You know, seeing him was more than I could stand. I had to cry. He told me he would stick by me, and I told him all I wanted him to do is to pray for me, that I didn't want him to spend one red cent on my behalf. I told him I didn't consider it necessary since whatever happens will be the will of God."

"Have you contacted a lawyer?" Wirges asked.

"It takes money to hire a lawyer, and I certainly haven't got any. My grandmother owns a little farm back home, but I would not have her dispose of it for me. After all, my family is not responsible for my troubles, so why should they wreck their own lives for me?"

One thing Hall wanted Wirges to stress and the first thing he wanted the reporter to write down was a message to the public concerning his sanity.

Detective Chief O.N. Martin. *Copyright Arkansas Democrat-Gazette.*

"I don't want people to think I'm crazy," he said.

They would reach the conclusion that I'm afraid to die. If I faked insanity now, the general reaction would be that I was looking for a way out. When I'm before the judge, I will tell him that I'm not insane. If I have to die for my crimes, I will die with the knowledge that I will meet my Maker. I have been saved and I know God will not turn me down. Why I committed these murders, I don't know, and no one except God has the answer.

Hall said he was arranging to have a history of his life published with half of the royalties going to the ghostwriter and the other half going into a trust fund for his two-year-old son. Then he proceeded to talk about other murders he had committed.

"The urge to kill came on me in 1938 while I was working on a ranch in Arizona. My boss was George Shoemaker. I drove a truck for him. Many Mexicans were employed on the ranch, and over a period of about a month, I killed ten of them. I killed them all to rob them."

"How did you do it?" Wirges pressed him for details. "How did you get away with that many murders?"

"It really was easy," Hall said. "I walked them out into the desert, never more than one at a time. I always had the difference, either a club or a pistol. After I had marched a victim into a remote section of the desert, I'd kill and rob him. Sometimes I'd beat him to death, and other times I'd shoot him. I never got more than fifty dollars from any one of them."

Bodies of migrant farm workers were sometimes discovered, but when one *was* found, no one seemed interested. After all, they figured, it was only a Mexican. Those who went missing created no great deal of excitement. It was assumed they had just left the country. From 1929 through 1937, as many as 400,000 Mexican migrant workers returned to their native land, either because of roundups and deportations by the Federal Bureau of Immigration or violence from vigilantes angered by the loss of jobs to the group, even though some of the workers were U.S. citizens themselves.

"I never felt bad about any of my killings," Hall said. "I always slept well."

He didn't remember the names of any of the ten Mexican workers, which wasn't surprising since he couldn't recall the names of his most recent victims in Arkansas when first questioned about those.

"Did you kill anybody else between 1938 and last September when you killed Fayrene?" Wirges asked.

Hall shook his head. "No. You see, I married a sweet country girl in 1939 and lived with her until a couple of years ago. I was a good boy all that time. I worked steadily and every dime I earned was gained honestly. When we separated, I went back to my old ways again. Some Oklahoma officers questioned me today, thinking I killed some people in that state, but they're wrong. I admit I pulled some fast ones in Oklahoma but no killings."

Hall didn't elaborate on those crimes but did tell of playing in a high-stakes poker game in New Orleans where he detected the dealer drawing cards from the bottom of the deck. He said he made a gun play and "took charge of the situation."

"My next killing after 1938 was in San Marcos, Texas, last December when I beat a man to rob him. I think I got about eighty dollars from him. I still saw him lying motionless four hours later."

The interview was interrupted frequently when Hall sought to substantiate a point by quoting the Bible.

"You know," he said, "There are some people who can't kill a chicken or a cat. I never was that way. I always could kill anything without compunction, but I never could stand to see anything suffer."

"How about your murder victims?" Wirges asked.

Hall shot back, "They never suffered a bit."

"They or their families might disagree with you on that."

"Well…" For once, Red was at a loss for words.

"What's your opinion of the police?"

"I always tried to cooperate with them. Many of them are swell fellas and, after all, an officer has a duty to perform just the same as anyone else. The officers who have handled my case have been gentlemen. In fact, every officer I've met since I was arrested has been kind and courteous. They're a swell bunch of fellas."

After Wirges left, Hall asked jailer George Higgins for stationery, envelopes and stamps, explaining he wanted to write "a few letters." Higgins gave him the supplies and a dull pencil. When Red made a mistake in his writing, he had a habit of licking the pencil's eraser before using it.

9

THE STATE VERSUS JAMES WAYBERN HALL

As Hall neared his day in court, the war in Europe was nearing its conclusion. Canadian forces had noticed the German SS and Gestapo troops were withdrawing to interior Germany for a last-ditch stand. The U.S. Army disclosed that one of its most valuable weapons in Europe was the German soldier's inability to keep his mouth shut. American commanders were amazed at the willingness of German POWs to divulge vital information. Whereas U.S. soldiers were drilled to give only their name, rank and serial number, their German counterparts shed their loyalty to a cause they knew was lost, a cause that many of them hadn't advocated in the first place. Their sentiments were mirrored by demoralized Germans still fighting in Europe. A Moscow radio broadcast reported that on the eastern front, a force of German Volkssturm troops (the People's Militia) whose commander refused to lead them into battle, were shot and killed by German regular army soldiers.

Among the people in Arkansas fervently yearning for an end to combat were the twenty-three thousand German and Italian prisoners of war who worked at thirty sites around the state, mostly in the delta, where they were bused in from the three main housing centers: Camp Robinson in North Little Rock, Camp Chaffee in Fort Smith and Camp Dermott in Chicot County. Besides doing chores in the camps, the POWs were put to work on farms to alleviate the agricultural manpower shortage that the state had experienced when thousands of rural youths went off to war. Edwin Pelz wrote a memoir about his time as a German POW in Arkansas. He had arrived during cotton picking season, and he recalled how each prisoner was required to pick 120 pounds of cotton every day. At the end of his first day, he had only 40 pounds and had to work in moonlight to meet the quota. His fellow captives helped him and told him their secret: collecting every rock and pebble they could lay their hands on and hiding them in the cotton sacks to make them weigh more. Life in the camps wasn't bad, though, according to Pelz. The prisoners could play sports and had decent shelter in army barracks, and with the eighty cents a day they earned, they could buy such things as cigarettes and candy. They also ate the same chow as the American soldiers, who got food that ordinary citizens could not buy due to rationing. By and large, Arkansans appreciated having the POWs to work on farms and in the timber industry, where there was also a labor shortage. However, some other segments of society resented the enemy presence on American soil, no matter what the reason. That hostility turned violent—just as the Allies were on the threshold of victory in Europe—when an unknown person fired a shotgun into a work camp at West Helena, wounding five Germans. Guards found two 16-gauge shells outside the fence. None of the prisoners was wounded seriously enough to require hospitalization, but the government considered closing the compound, much to the dismay of members of the Phillips County Farmers Association. They intended to increase the quota of cotton picked to 150 pounds per prisoner per day during the autumn harvest.

While farmers were hoping for bumper crops in the fall, Red Hall was hoping for a fair trial. He would be fighting in court not only before a judge and jury but also before the court of public opinion. He had become a household name in many Arkansas communities. Nowhere more so than Enola. Almost everyone there had seen him at one time or another. They spoke of him as if he were a mythic creature, a boogeyman, Raw Head and Bloody Bones himself. Children on their way to school or to the store would tease and scare each other when they passed thickets.

"You better watch out! Red Hall may be in there. He'll getcha!"

Sometimes a cohort would leap from behind the bushes and pounce on their playmates. Even those who laughed at the prank often flinched. Others screamed and ran away.

Despite confessing to more than a dozen murders in other states, Hall would never be tried for any of them. Having committed slayings in several different areas of Arkansas, he could have been charged for any one of those crimes in the corresponding court venue, but Pulaski County prosecuting attorney Sam Robinson was at the head of the line.

POWs housed at Camp Robinson. *Arkansas National Guard Archives*.

He arraigned Hall for first-degree murder in the death of Fayrene. It was thought to be the strongest case against him. If the trial resulted in a capital punishment decree, additional charges would not be needed. If the court didn't hand down the death penalty, however, the other jurisdictions had the right to try Hall. This was in accordance with a statute passed about thirty years earlier after a quadruple murderer had been given a sentence of life imprisonment and then, in a different trial, given death; he had to serve life before being executed.

On March 26, 1945, Robinson formally charged Hall with murder in the first degree, stating that "on the fourteenth day of September 1944, James Waybern Hall, willfully and maliciously, and after premeditation and deliberation with an unlawful and felonious intent, did assault, kill and murder Fayrene Clemmons Hall."

The trial would take place in the First Division Circuit Court in the Pulaski County Courthouse. This building, still in existence today, has an architectural dual personality. Part of it, constructed in the late 1880s, is in the elaborate Romanesque style with terra-cotta trim and small gables between corner turrets. A clock tower tops the two-story rotunda. The original clock was destroyed in a storm in 1961 but was replaced in 1995. The second part of the courthouse, added in 1914, is a sedate, boxy rendering of the Beaux-Arts design made from Batesville limestone and marble. The combined edifices and a small park-like area cover an entire city block, bounded by South Spring Street, West Markham, West Second and South Broadway.

As Red had told Joe Wirges, he was financially unable to hire a lawyer, so circuit judge Gus Fulk appointed M.V. Moody to represent the accused.

The following day, Red made his first trip to the Tucker State Prison Farm. The prison would gain much notoriety in the late 1960s for its use of a torture device known as the "Tucker Telephone." The Tucker Telephone was an old-fashioned crank telephone wired with two batteries. Guards or prison trusties would attach electrodes to a prisoner's big toe and genitals and then turn the crank, passing an electrical charge through the inmate's body. Governor Winthrop Rockefeller, after entering office in 1967, sought to put an end to such barbarities and appointed Thomas Murton as the new superintendent. The state penitentiary became the Arkansas Department of Corrections (ADC) in 1968, and it was early that year that Murton announced to the public that human remains had been found buried on prison property. Eventually, the skeletons totaled two hundred. The Rockefeller administration fired Murton for divulging news about the discoveries before first informing the state. In one case, it was claimed that the legs of the deceased had been broken in order for the body to fit inside a wooden box. The state said the burial site was a pauper's grave for inmates whose bodies were not claimed by relatives. In 1970, Judge J. Smith Henley ruled the entire state's prison system violated the Eighth Amendment to the Constitution, which bans the use of cruel and unusual punishment. He also said the ADC interfered with prisoners' access to the court system. Only in 1973 did Henley release the ADC from his jurisdiction because of improvements that had been accomplished.

Sheriff Caple and two deputies, W.E. Johnson and Ray Hayes, transferred Hall to Tucker, where he was put in a death cell with orders that peace officers but no newspapermen be permitted to talk to him.

Red's stay at Tucker was short, just one night, because Judge Fulk ordered that he undergo a thirty-day mental observation at the State Hospital for Nervous Diseases. The decision came at the behest of M.V. Moody, laying the groundwork for an insanity plea. The hospital admitted Hall at 3:00 p.m., but he was returned to the county jail later that evening. Dr. A.C. Kolb, hospital superintendent, said the criminal ward was inadequate to hold Hall or any other prisoner. Ordinarily, a lawbreaker placed in the hospital

The Pulaski County Courthouse where Hall's trial took place. *Photo by the author.*

for observation remained day and night, but Kolb declined to accept the responsibility of keeping Hall that night. The hospital never had a ward deemed escape-proof despite repeated efforts to obtain such facilities. Bowing to the doctor's safety issues, the ASP kept Hall in jail during the night, delivered him to the hospital every morning, stood guard over him all day and returned him to his jail cell at night. To allay Captain Scroggin's concerns that such an arrangement would be a hardship on the ASP by taking an officer from other duties, Kolb promised to finish the evaluation within the thirty-day period. True to his word, he completed the mental examination well within the allotted time, submitting his findings after only twenty days. In a letter to Judge Fulk, he wrote, in part, "(1.) It is my opinion that James Waybern Hall is without psychosis, that is, sane and legally responsible for his acts, at the time of this examination, and (2.) It is my

Arkansas State Hospital for Nervous Diseases where judge sent Hall for psychiatric evaluation. *Courtesy University of Central Arkansas Archives.*

opinion that James Waybern Hall was without psychosis, that is, sane and legally responsible for his acts at the time of the alleged commission of the crime of murder for which he is charged."

"I guess I'll get the electric chair," Red told reporters, "But it don't matter. That would be better than life imprisonment."

On the eve of his trial, he spent a quiet day talking with his father and his lawyer. They were his only visitors.

The court had summoned forty witnesses to testify against him and twenty-four in support of his defense. Dr. Kolb received subpoenas from both sides. Taking the advice of counsel, Hall had changed his mind about his mental state. Instead of telling the court he was sane, he went along with Moody's assertion that he wasn't guilty by reason of insanity. He also reversed himself on his admission of guilt, alleging the police had coerced the confession out of him, his opinion of them as a "swell bunch of fellas" notwithstanding.

On the same day that Red's trial convened, bold print headlines in newspapers everywhere heralded the surrender of Nazi Germany. Public emotions across the United States were a mixture of joy and relief. But inside the First Division Circuit Court in Little Rock, a somber air prevailed when the clerk called the gathering to order. Judge Lawrence C. Auten took his seat behind the bench precisely at 10:00 a.m. and voir dire began. In questioning potential jurors, Prosecutor Robinson emphasized their viewpoints about capital punishment. Several said they were opposed to the death penalty but would return a guilty verdict if evidence justified it. Defense Attorney Moody asked their opinion of an insanity plea. Both lawyers posed questions about rendering a verdict based on circumstantial evidence. Most of those excused by the court said they already had formed an opinion about Hall's guilt or innocence and would not be able to serve without bias. Of the forty-seven veniremen questioned, seventeen were excused by Judge Auten, eleven by Moody and seven by the prosecutor. The court was in recess from noon to 1:30 p.m., and the all-male jury was impaneled two hours later. Those who were chosen included a salesman, a grocer, a business executive and four retired railroad employees, as well as a retiree from the Railway Express Agency. What a coincidence that so many were connected to the train industry. For Red, hopping a freight was the next best thing to hitching. Well-groomed and in a sociable mood, he showed no trace of nervousness throughout the proceedings. He smiled frequently and had a habit of slinging one leg over the chair arm and swinging it back and forth, the very picture of nonchalance.

Judge Auten adjourned the trial, and the jury was sequestered with Deputy Sheriffs Bob Lusby and Robert Wells in charge of the group.

Many of the reporters covering the trial withdrew to a bar located in the Hotel Marion on Markham Street. The Marion was one of Arkansas's most famous landmarks. In existence since 1907, the five-hundred-room building was quite swanky. Bellboys wore green suits to match the green carpet, and a marble fishpond was the focal point in the lobby. Harry Truman, Helen Keller and Will Rogers were among the people who had signed the guestbook over the years. The cocktail lounge was called the Gar Hole, named for the alligator gar, a freshwater fish once plentiful in the tributaries up and down the Mississippi River Valley, including the White River in Arkansas. Proud fisherman often mounted their prize catches, and such was the case with the perfect specimen on the wall behind the bar at the Marion. The watering hole at the most elegant hotel in Little Rock attracted reporters because it was a top spot for politicians to negotiate deals, and anywhere you have a politician, chances are you have a news lead. It was also just a few blocks from the Pulaski County Courthouse, another source of fodder for the Fourth Estate.

The Hotel Marion, a ritzy establishment and home of the Gar Hole, a bar frequented by reporters and politicians. *Library of Congress*.

When court reconvened at 9:00 a.m. the next day, Robinson's opening statement and Moody's reaction to it set the tone for the trial because the defense attorney's objections were as numerous as they were pointless, delaying tactics being just another way to hold the executioner at bay.

Robinson began. "The defendant took his wife, Fayrene Hall, out near the riverbank on the other side of the Riverside Golf Course and murdered her."

"I want to object to that statement," Moody said, "That he did murder her."

"Objection overruled," Judge Auten said. "The prosecuting attorney is stating what is an allegation."

Robinson continued, "There he murdered his wife and left her body—"

"Object to that statement."

"Overruled."

"—thinking that the body would be devoured by dogs and hogs and possums—"

"We object to that statement," Moody spoke for his client.

Auten said, "The State is just presenting what he expects to prove."

Moody disagreed. "He couldn't expect to prove that the body was devoured by dogs and hogs."

"Overruled."

Robinson went on. "This is one of the most dastardly crimes ever committed in this county or the country—"

"I object to his making his case at this time," Moody said.

"Overruled."

Robinson again. "This is a case of deliberate, pre-meditated murder—"

"Objection."

"Overruled."

Robinson was resolute. "The defendant has pleaded not guilty by reason of insanity. Gentlemen of the jury, he does not have a single solitary symptom of insanity."

"Objection," Moody said and tried to nullify the entirety of his opponent's narrative. "I object to his opening statement."

"Mr. Moody," Auten explained patiently, "The defendant has pleaded not guilty by reason of insanity, and the prosecuting attorney has a right to make a statement relative to that. Don't argue."

Robinson persevered. "I was just stating that we are going to prove by evidence—"

"I object to that arguing part," Moody said, slipping in a rebuke to the judge himself.

At this time, Auten asked Robinson, Moody and the defendant to join him in chambers so he could hear disputes from both sides of the debate.

"Your Honor," Robinson said, "The State proposes to prove that the defendant made a confession to the officers that he killed his wife, Fay Clemmons Hall, and led the officers to where he left the body, where the remains of the body were found."

"Is that a written confession?" Auten asked.

"No, sir," Robinson conceded but explained that Hall had confessed to lawmen and to the court-appointed psychiatrist. "If it is objected to by the defendant, we will put on our testimony now as to the fact that the confession was voluntary in both instances."

Auten looked at Moody. "I believe you stated that you want to object?"

"I object to any confession at all."

"Your Honor," an exasperated Robinson said, "If Mr. Moody continues to object to every fraction of a statement I make, this won't be the trial of the century, but it may last a century."

While still in judge's chambers, the court allowed Robinson to call in witnesses who had been present during the times that Hall had spoken of killing his wife and other victims. The first person summoned was Detective Judd, whose extensive testimony filled twenty-eight pages of the trial transcript. He answered questions from both counsels regarding physical evidence that had been gathered and about circumstances surrounding Hall's arrest and interrogation. He said that Hall had confessed freely and willingly both at the police station and during the trips to the crime scenes.

At the conclusion of Judd's testimony, Robinson sought to avoid tedious and redundant dialogue. "May it please the court," he said, "I have any number of witnesses—probably seven or eight—I can put on the stand to the effect that the confession was not coerced, that it was entirely voluntary. I don't know what evidence Mr. Moody has to the contrary at all, but simply for the purpose of shortening this hearing, I would like it to be agreed that I could rest at this time and put the other witnesses on in rebuttal if necessary."

After a brief conference with his client, Moody asked Hall to tell why the confession should be suppressed, and the defendant proceeded to complain about the harsh treatment he had received at the hands of his captors.

"You heard Mr. Judd testify?" Moody asked.

"Yes, sir."

"About there had been no abuse to you?"

"Yes, sir."

"Had there been?"

"Yes, sir."

"Describe that for me. Tell the Court."

"A man named Oliphant of the State Police called me a low-down son-of-a-bitch and kicked me in the seat of my pants. Then they swarmed around me, and I was threatened continually as they questioned me."

Robinson cross-examined. "Who threatened you?"

"Peterson, Oliphant, Sims, and Judd. I was abused by language and drug around by handcuffs."

"Drug around?"

"Yes, sir. Led around."

"You were handcuffed to officers?"

"Yes, sir."

"Did they drag you?"

"It was either keep up or be dragged."

"You mean the officers were walking that fast?"

"If I didn't go on, well—"

"You were pulling back?"

"No, because the handcuffs would hurt my wrists."

"It would equally hurt the officers' wrists, would it not?"

"They led me."

"So they didn't drag you?"

"Not as if I were dead, no. I didn't lay down and let them drag me."

"You meant you were handcuffed and went along. Is that it?"

"Yes, sir."

During redirect, Moody asked Hall, "Did you murder your wife?"

"No, sir."

"Do you know where she is?"

"No, sir."

Questioned again by Robinson, Hall denied ever being at the crime scenes until taken there by police: "All I knew about the crime scenes was what I read in the newspapers. Peterson said they were going to send me to the chair. He said he would 'stomp hell out of me,' if I didn't take him to the places and I would be sorry if I didn't. He said if I didn't confess, they would get my kinfolks and they would have to enlarge the Faulkner County Jail to hold 'em all. I had nothing else to resort to."

Robinson called Peterson, Judd, Oliphant and Joe Wirges to refute the allegations of abuse, and all swore that they were present when Hall confessed and that at no time was he threatened, cursed, abused, kicked, called foul names or mistreated in any way and that no hope of reward was held out to him.

"That's the State's case on that question," Robinson concluded.

Auten laid down one ground rule. "I might say here, Mr. Moody, to make it clear, that the Court will not admit any part of a confession which refers to other alleged crimes that the defendant purportedly stated he committed. It will be confined solely to the crime with which he is charged here, the unlawful killing of his wife as set forth in the indictment. Should the State either inadvertently or otherwise bring it out, the Court will immediately stop them. I want to call this to your attention because should your cross-examination at any time bring it out, then it would be putting something else in issue, and the Court wants to protect the defendant's rights all the way through. I want to caution you should the defense bring out anything relative to other crimes, then the matter is open for cross-examination and it would be proper testimony."

"It has never been shown that a murder has been committed at all," Moody said.

"The State will have to prove the corpus delicti," Auten assured him.

Moody went on, "I object to any so-called confession drawn from my client by the court-appointed psychiatrist. Anything the defendant said falls under doctor/patient privilege and, therefore, cannot be used against him."

As long as the insanity defense has been around, legal and psychiatric scholars have wrestled with the scope of confidentiality in criminal cases. The general consensus, however, is that the psychiatrist/patient privilege does not exist when the communication is during a court-ordered exam and the patient's mental health is at issue in the case. Auten based his ruling on this precedent and issued his decision at once.

"I am admitting both confessions under proper instructions to the jury that they will be the judges of the fact as to whether the confessions were voluntary, and the burden is on the State to convince them. It now becomes a fact for the jury to determine."

When the trial resumed in the courtroom, Moody made his opening statement to the jury, summarizing the position of the defense.

"You will be told by prosecution witnesses that Mr. Hall confessed to killing his wife, but I state to you, gentlemen of the jury, that such a confession, if in fact there was one, was obtained through coercion. Mr. Robinson can probably prove statements concerning the Halls' visit to the dance hall on the fourteenth of September, the night the State charges Mrs. Hall was killed, but the State will be unable to prove that Mrs. Hall is dead. No person knows whether Fayrene Hall is alive or dead today. All through this case, you will find that it cannot be proved that she is not living. However, if you think enough proof exists to conclude that Hall killed Fay, you will then have to consider the question of his sanity. We will show by the best psychiatrists in the country that Mr. Hall is insane."

After a ninety-minute recess for lunch, spectators crowded back into the courtroom. Because public interest in the trial was so great, seats were at a premium and quickly filled to capacity. Auten asked all standing spectators to leave.

Hall chatted with bystanders and was unperturbed when a skull, jawbone, shoes, dress and patch of hair and scalp were placed on the court clerk's table. He glanced at them several times without changing his expression.

The prosecution's first witness was a clean-shaven and well-dressed Cecil Foster, who testified to finding a skull while he was looking for firewood in the pasture near his house past the Riverside Golf Course. He recalled the date was the fifth of January, remembering it because it was the Friday before he started a new job as a driver for England Brothers Truck Line.

"What did you do with the skull?" Robinson asked.

Foster said, "First thing, I drove along in the wagon and I said, 'I believe there's a skull.' I took it to the house, and it laid there in the wagon for a couple of days or more before I throwed it in the loft."

Foster then identified the skull on the clerk's table, and Robinson introduced it as Exhibit 1.

During cross-examination, Moody attempted to prove that the skull could have come from somewhere else.

"You made no report of finding the skull?"

"No, sir," Foster said.

"Why didn't you?"

"I figured it had washed in there during high water."

"Is it very frequent that you have things wash up there on that piece of property after high water? Driftwood and the like?"

"Yes, sir."

"You went down when you saw the officers in your pasture?"

"Yes, sir."

"Did you know they were officers?"

"No, I didn't know who they was."

"Why did you go down there?"

"I was sitting in the house, reading the paper, and one of my children seen them and told me, and I went over to the pasture."

"Did you know they were looking for anything?"

"I read in the papers they was going to search for this woman's body."

"You were well aware of what they were doing down there?"

"I had an idea that's what they were looking for."

"Of your own knowledge, you believed that's what they were looking for because you read the papers?"

"Yes, sir."

"That they would be looking for the body?"

"Yes, sir."

"You read it in the paper?"

"Yes, sir."

"You thought they were looking for a body?"

"Yes, sir."

"You went down there?"

"Yes, sir. I met those people and asked them what they was looking for, and they told me."

"What did they tell you?"

"They told me they was looking for the Hall boy's wife's body."

"They were looking for a skeleton?"

"Body is what they told me."

"You told them about the skull?"

"Yes, sir."

"Who went with you to retrieve the skull?"

"No one."

"Who did you hand the skull to when you came back to the pasture?"

"I couldn't tell you. I didn't know nobody."

"Did you hand it to a man, woman or child?"

"I don't know. It was someone."

Moody continued to question the witness with such specificity that Judge Auten intervened.

"Mr. Moody, I don't know for what purpose these questions are. The man testified he found this skull and that's all he says he knows about it. I don't want to interrupt you, but just tell the Court the purpose of further such interrogation. I don't see it is of any value."

Moody feigned innocent ignorance. "The Court objects to my asking that question?"

"The Court objects to the repetition."

Undaunted, Moody continued with the witness. "I asked you in general, you found a skull?"

"Yes, sir."

"Did you know it was the skull of a human?"

"Yes."

"Why didn't you make a report that you had discovered a skull up there?"

"I didn't think but what it had washed in there during the overflow. I never thought nothing about it."

"You never thought about it being a human skull?"

"I thought they had just drowned and washed in during the high water."

"You don't know but what it was washed in there, do you?"

"I don't know."

After Foster was excused, Robinson called Patrolman Allen to the stand. The prosecutor picked up the jawbone from among the exhibits on the clerk's table and held it out for the witness and jurors to see. Allen identified it as the one he found on the riverbank.

In cross-examination, Moody asked about the ground where they had searched for the remains.

"Can this land be flooded?"

"Yes, sir," Allen said. "It has been flooded but not in the last year."

"It wasn't flooded in 1944?"

"It wasn't flooded *there*."

"Were you and your passengers the first people to reach this place?"

"No, sir. Some other men in our party were there."

"They had beat you there?"

"Yes, sir."

"How did you know where you were going?"

"Red was showing us where to go."

"Was he in the car with you?"

"No, he was in the lead car with Peterson, and the rest of us followed them."

During a short recess, Hall's parents entered the courtroom and, for the duration of the day, sat by their son at his counsel's table. They didn't talk much among themselves but bowed their heads when the elder Mr. Hall said a prayer. Only those nearest to them could hear the devotional.

When the trial resumed, Detectives Judd and then Peterson took the stand and identified the other human remains and clothing, and Robinson subsequently entered the items into evidence.

The judge's objection to Moody's monotonous questions hadn't fazed the attorney. Again and again, he delved for minute details by asking each witness the same questions; who rode with whom in what car to the alleged crime scene, who found what and where. The lengthy testimony filled thirty-five pages of the trial transcript.

Pulaski County coroner Dr. Howard Dishongh testified that the remains were human, "most likely a woman, but I couldn't say for sure."

The next subpoenaed witness, Muriel Stevenson, took the stand and identified the clothing and jawbone as that of Fay's. She recognized the red dress immediately because of the unusual buttons, but both attorneys had other questions for her as well.

"Did you know Fayrene Clemmons Hall in her lifetime?" Robinson asked.

"Sure did," Muriel said.

"Were you in any way related to her?"

"My husband is her half brother."

"Do you remember the time of her disappearance?"

"It was Thursday, I think, the fourteenth of September."

"When is the last time *you* saw her prior to that day?"

"I saw her the tenth of September."

"How do you know it was the tenth of September?"

"Because the next day, I sent my husband's little niece to school for the first time."

"What day did school start?"

"The eleventh of September."

"Then it was on Sunday the tenth of September the last time you ever saw her?"

"Yes, sir."

"Was she in good health?"

"Yes, sir, she was."

"Did you see the defendant on that same day?"

"Sure did."

"When was the next time you talked with the defendant after that?"

"I don't know the exact date. I talked with him on the phone. I asked to speak to Fay."

"Was it the following week?"

"It was on Friday morning, I think."

"Following the tenth of September?"

"Yes, sir."

"What did he tell you?"

"He said she left him Thursday night."

"Did he say anything about where her clothes were?"

"He said she left in such a hurry that she didn't pack and take them with her."

"You knew Fay Hall well?"

"I think I knew her pretty well. She lived with us for a while."

"How long had you known her?"

"Six years."

"Did you ever notice her lower teeth?"

"Yes, sir."

Robinson picked up the jawbone and held it for the witness' inspection.

"Can you say whether or not the teeth in this jawbone introduced into evidence—"

"I object to that," Moody said. "She hasn't stated whose bone it is."

Robinson responded, "I haven't finished the question yet."

Addressing Moody, Judge Auten said, "You will have to wait until he finishes the question."

Robinson continued with the witness. "You had come in contact with her many times?"

"That's right."

"State whether or not her tooth lapped over as it does in this jawbone."

The prosecutor indicated the distinctive dental flaw to which he was referring.
"It did."

"Your Honor, I want to pass the jawbone around for the jury to examine it."

Moody stood up. "I object to the introduction of that."

"It has already been introduced," Auten said. "Objection overruled."

After the defense exceptions were noted and made a part of the record, the prosecution addressed the witness again.

"What color was her hair?"

"It was a shade darker than mine," Muriel said.

"Did it happen to be the color of the hair on that table?"

Robinson pointed to the patch of hair.

"Yes, sir."

Moody admonished counsel. "Don't lead the witness."

"I'm not leading the witness," Robinson protested.

"You're putting words in her mouth," Moody said.

Judge Auten interceded as if he were separating two children fighting over a toy. "I am going to ask both of you not to carry on conversations between yourselves. Make your objections to the Court."

Robinson continued. "Do you recognize these shoes that have been introduced into evidence?"

"I do."

"Who do you recognize them as having belonged to?"

"Fayrene Hall."

Robinson had no more questions for the witness, so Moody began his cross-examination, challenging Muriel's identification of the jawbone.

"Why do you recognize it as being hers?"

"By the buck tooth."

"Have you ever seen her jawbone prior to this?"

"No, but I've seen her teeth many times."

"Have you examined the jawbone prior?"

"I have examined the teeth."

"Then is that Mrs. Hall's jaw?"

"I think it is."

"Is it, or isn't it?"

"It is."

"Are you positive about the shoes?"

"Yes, sir."

Moody addressed the judge saying, "I want to introduce the shoes."

"They are already introduced," Auten reminded him.

"I want the jury to see the shoes," Moody said, handing them to the jury foreman, V.E. Cooke, who passed them around.

Moody spoke to the witness, "You know that is her skull, you know these are her shoes, you know that is her hair."

"Wait a minute," Robinson interrupted.

"She didn't know about the skull," Auten said. "She identified the other articles. Let her answer each question individually."

But Moody was through and turned the witness back to Robinson for redirect examination.

"With reference to these shoes, you saw the shoes the day she bought them?"

"Yes, sir. I was with her when she bought them, and then I saw them again on Sunday."

"The Sunday before she disappeared on Thursday."

"That's right."

"You saw them on Sunday?"

"She put them on, and they hurt her feet."

With no more questions for her, the witness was excused.

The next person sworn in was Fay's friend Katy Bryant, whose name had since become Mrs. Clyde Green after her marriage on December 30, 1944. At the time of the trial, she lived in Doniphan, Missouri, and was returning to Little Rock to testify against Hall. She related the events of the night she had accompanied him and Fay to the Rainbow Garden and how the evening had ended on such a sour note due to Red Hall's ill temper.

"Have you ever seen Fay Hall from that hour to this?" Robinson asked.

"No, I haven't."

"Do you know what kind of dress she had on that night?"

"Yes, sir. A red dress, a two-piece."

"Have you had occasion to look at the remains of this dress?"

Robinson indicated the dress scraps on the clerk's table. He picked up the remnant of clothing with care out of respect for the woman who had worn it ostensibly for an evening of fun and frivolity, never guessing it would serve as her shroud.

"Yes, I've seen that dress."

"Does this appear to be the dress she had on?"

"Yes, sir, that's the dress."

"How do you identify it?"

"By the buttons."

"These are buttons with little chains with a thing on the end that looks like a nail, and they fasten in that manner?" Robinson demonstrated how the closure worked.

"Yes, sir."

"Was that the dress she had on that night?"

"Yes, sir."

Moody cross-examined the witness, challenging her memory. "It's just a rag now. Are you positive these are the clothes that Fayrene Clemmons Hall wore?"

"Yes, sir."

"This is the first time you've seen them since that night—when was that?"

"It was Thursday or Friday night."

"In what month?"

"In August."

Moody pounced on this contradiction; everyone else, including Red, had stated that Fay disappeared in September.

"Was that the first of August or the last?" Moody asked.

"I wouldn't be positive."

"But it was a Thursday or Friday night in August 1944?"

"It was ladies' night at the Rainbow."

"Ladies' night at the Rainbow in August 1944, but you don't remember what date."

"No, sir."

"Would you say the first of the month or the end of the month or sometime in the middle of the month?"

"I wouldn't say. I'm not positive."

"You cannot be positive about this dress."

"Yes, that's the dress she had on," Katy stuck to her guns about the clothing.

"You know it," Moody pressed her.

"Yes, sir."

"As positive of that as any other testimony you have given?"

"Yes, sir. That's the dress."

Robinson approached the witness for redirect.

"You saw the dress and observed the peculiar fasteners?"

"Yes, sir. That's what I noticed about it. We were talking about it."

"Of course, you have no way of fixing the date?"

"No, I wouldn't say what date it was."

After the conclusion of Katy's testimony, Robinson called reporter Agnes Watson to the stand next, and she told the jury she had been present when searchers found the jawbone near the Riverside Golf Course.

"Hall said he could tell the jawbone was that of his wife's because of one overlapping tooth," Watson said. "He was sure in his description of those teeth."

Moody had no questions, and the witness was excused.

Dorothy Barton testified about the short time she had known Fay, and then W.A. Woods testified.

"Mr. Woods, will you please tell the court how you knew the Halls?" Robinson asked.

"They were tenants of mine. They rented an apartment from me."

"Were they living there at the time Mrs. Hall disappeared?"

"Yes, sir."

"Did the defendant say anything to you about her absence?" Robinson asked.

"Yes, sir."

"What did he tell you?"

"He told me she had gone east. He supposed she was meeting a friend of hers she used to know."

"After she disappeared, were her clothes still there?"

"Yes, sir."

"They remained there?"

"Yes, sir."

Woods also established the time of Fay's disappearance at some time in September 1944. He said the Halls moved into the apartment on August 25, 1944, and Red moved out around the twelfth or fourteenth of October.

When A.Z. Clemmons took the stand, a reverent silence filled the courtroom. Though Robinson addressed the witness in a subdued tone, every word was as clear as a mockingbird's song on a midsummer night. Clemmons's responses were equally distinct but filled with the melancholy that only parents of a dead child can understand. Robinson would have spared Clemmons the ordeal of testifying, but a positive identification of the exhibits was necessary to prove false the defense's claim that Fay's body was never found.

"Have you examined the hair there before you that has been introduced in evidence?" Robinson asked, pointing to the exhibits. "Those shoes, jawbone and teeth?"

"Yes, sir."

"Can you identify those shoes?"

"Yes, sir. They were Fay's."

"Can you identify the hair?"

"Yes, sir. It was Fay's."

"How about the teeth? You observe how the tooth overlaps the other?"

"Yes, sir."

"Did your daughter, Fay, resemble you?"

"Yes, sir."

"I object," Moody interrupted. "I can see no reason for that question."

"Overruled."

"You say the girl resembled you?" Robinson continued.

"Yes, sir."

"Let's see your lower teeth. Were her lower teeth similar to yours?"

"Just like."

"Step down in front of the jury, please."

Moody objected, but the court allowed the demonstration, to which Moody said, facetiously, "Then we have to exhibit his skull."

"The Court will pass on that," Auten replied in all seriousness. "If you want to introduce his skull, you can on cross-examination."

Clemmons walked in front of the jury and pulled his lower lip down to show the same buck tooth that was visible on the jawbone in evidence.

Moody's cross-examination was brief. Clemmons restated with certainty that the items on exhibit belonged to Fay. After he stepped down, his wife took the stand. Mourning lined her face as she verified that Fay had married Hall in March 1944.

"Do you know whether or not they went to Oregon?" Robinson asked.

"Yes, sir. They went to Oregon."

"You heard from them while they were out there?"

"Yes, sir."

"Did she write while she was in Oregon?"

"Yes, sir. I think I have the letters."

"Then when she was away, she wrote to you frequently?"

"They wasn't in Oregon no time it seemed, until they had got there and come back, and I got two letters and a card from her. They stayed with us a week after they came back."

"When was the last time you saw your daughter Fay?"

"The eleventh of September."

"Where did you see her?"

"She was at my house."

"Was this defendant Hall with her?"

"Yes, sir."

"Have you seen her from that day to this?"

"No, sir. It was the last time I ever saw her."

"From the day she was at your farm on the eleventh of September, you haven't heard a word?"

"Nothing. Not a word from her since."

Mrs. Clemmons also identified the exhibits as being Fay's.

Moody's cross-examination merely sought to establish a timeline of events before the witness was excused. Chief Martin was the next to be sworn in, but after Robinson attempted to open a line of questioning about the .38 pistol found in Hall's rented room, Moody objected. The primary parties were called into judge's chambers, where they took up the matter. Because Hall admitted he had beaten Fay to death, the gun had no bearing on the case. It would have opened the door to the other murders Hall had committed, and it had already been agreed that those crimes were off limits. The gun, therefore, was inadmissible.

Returning to the courtroom, Robinson recalled Harold Judd as his next witness, and Judd told of Hall confessing he had killed Fay with his hands and led the officers to her decomposed body. Moody's cross-examination was mainly an attempt to cast doubt on the confession being voluntary. Peterson, Oliphant, Wirges and Sims followed Judd, and their testimony was basically the same as they had presented in chambers.

Oliphant testified, "He said he killed her and could take us to the spot where he left the body."

Sims told the court, "He said he killed her with his hands by a couple of licks under the jaw."

The remainder of the trial focused on Hall's mental state. Robinson called Dr. Kolb to the stand. Over numerous objections by Moody, Kolb read from a stenographic copy of the sessions he had conducted with Hall.

"Question: 'Did you have a feeling of regret after killing your wife?'"

"Answer: 'In a way I did and in a way I didn't, but it was about the only decision to be made at that time. I considered that if I never told anyone what happened, nobody would ever know, and I considered that the body would never be discovered. I figured it would soon be devoured by cats and other animals and the water from the river.'"

Moody began the cross-examination.

"Will you read further on where you left off there a minute ago?"

Kolb obliged.

"Question: 'Did you worry about it?'"

"Answer: 'No.'"

"Question: 'Did you have a feeling of relief following the killing of your wife?'"

"Answer: 'No.'"

"Question: 'No sexual pleasure?'"

"Answer: 'No. I felt it another burden off my hands. She hadn't been anything but trouble during the time we were married, and I felt it another object out of my way.'"

"Question: 'And you had no feeling of regret?'"

"Answer: 'No.'"

"Question: 'And that was the first human life you had taken, unless the Negro woman died—'"

"That's all right," Moody interrupted. "Dr. Kolb, did you coerce the boy into making the statement?"

"Absolutely not."

Moody tried to clarify the relationship between Kolb and Hall in an effort to sway the jury's opinion, that Hall confessed to the doctor in confidence as a patient.

"You didn't examine the boy for the purpose of any treatment at all?"

"No, sir, I did not."

"You examined him for the purpose of testimony?"

"To determine his mental condition and make a report to the court on the findings of that examination."

"You didn't treat him?"

"No, sir. I was not called on to."

"You didn't examine him for the purpose of treating?"

"One day, he complained of a headache, and I gave him a couple of aspirin, but that was not the purpose of his being sent to the hospital."

Moody repeated the same questions and got the same answers, and then he advanced toward the witness.

"Isn't it a fact that you were prejudiced toward Mr. Hall?"

"Mr. Moody, I am under oath. I have no interest whatsoever in this case, and under my oath, I state without equivocation, I have no prejudice whatever against the man. I am not receiving one cent for appearing in court."

Moody shook a finger at Kolb. "Weren't you so prejudiced against this man you refused to let him stay in the hospital under this court's order?"

"Mr. Moody, refusal to keep this man in the hospital was not based on prejudice whatsoever. It was based on the fact that the hospital is not an escape-proof institution, and from the newspaper accounts, we had a dangerous man to deal with and for that reason only, I told the court I could not be responsible for keeping him overnight. A few months ago, we had a case—"

"I don't care about any other case. How many other men have you refused when you had an order from the court?"

"This is the first case, but it was based on a recent experience I had out there with another——"

"Don't tell me anything," Moody said.

Auten interjected, "I am going to have to interrupt here out of perfect fairness to the State and Defendant both. Dr. Kolb asked this court for permission to lodge the defendant at night in the County Jail, and that permission was granted. If you ask why the witness does a thing, you have to let him give the reason. You can't shut him off. If you want to ask a question, he is entitled to explain himself."

Moody addressed the witness again, "You say you had read the newspapers until you had become so prejudiced——"

Robinson cut in, speaking to Moody. "I have let this go along without making any objection, but it looks like I have to. Dr. Kolb made no such statement as that."

"Objection sustained."

"Why did you refuse to accept him at the hospital?" Moody asked.

"Before the defendant was sent out there, I asked Judge Auten if I could be permitted to return him to jail at night, that the hospital criminal ward was not escape proof. We had an unhappy experience along that line which I think I ought to explain."

"I don't care," Moody said with a condescending wave of his hand.

"Go ahead and explain why," Auten instructed Kolb.

"We had a man——"

"Objection," Moody said.

"Overruled."

"That has no bearing on this case," Moody argued.

"Overruled for this reason: You think the doctor is prejudiced for not taking the man in at the hospital. Since you have put that in issue, the doctor has a right to explain."

"I don't care anything about his explanation at all," Moody said, dismissively.

And with that, the witness was excused.

Hall, who had been looking a little bored, appeared to enjoy his lawyer's shenanigans.

Robinson then recalled Detective Peterson to the stand.

"Did Hall say why he killed his wife?"

"He did."

"What did he say about that?"

"He made two different statements."

"What did he say first?"

"He said she fooled away too much of his money."

"Later on, did he make a different statement as to why he killed her?"

"He did."

"What did he say then?"

"He said she had been on some trips with him out West, in the western states, and had too much on him."

After a brief cross-examination by Moody, Robinson rested. "That's the State's case, may it please the court."

"Mr. Moody," Auten said. "Due to the late hour, I'm calling a halt to the proceedings until tomorrow at which time you may begin your argument for the defense." Turning to the jury, the judge reminded them not to discuss the case. "Enjoy your supper and get some sleep."

Auten then told all of the spectators to remain in their seats as members of the jury, accompanied by the deputy sheriffs, filed out of the courtroom.

Revelers were still crowding the streets and sidewalks, celebrating the end of Hitler's war on humanity. Nearly 300,000 German troops had started their march homeward from Denmark in miles-long columns along the main roads. Just two months earlier, Nazis had banned the Danish newspaper *Hornholms Avis* for printing a line from Rudyard Kipling's renowned poem *Mandalay*. "Come you back, you British soldier; come you back to Mandalay!" The defeated Germans were transporting their luggage on wheelbarrows and in perambulators and other makeshift vehicles. They had burned official papers and destroyed all hand grenades. Supposedly. All their weapons were being left at the border. Supposedly. In truth, many of the soldiers—especially those who had been forced to fight or else be shot—just threw their weapons down on the ground, much to the delight of Danish schoolchildren. One little boy took a discarded German Luger to class and was showing it off, until the teacher confiscated it. A young student by the name of Anna Marie picked up a German machine gun. She and some friends took turns firing the weapon from a bridge over a stream. When she recounted the experience sixty years later, her face still glowed with a bright smile at the memory of mischievous triumph.

The third day of Red Hall's trial began in judge's chambers with Moody moving for a directed verdict of acquittal on the grounds that not enough proof had been shown to declare Fay Hall was dead, but Auten denied the request.

Back in the courtroom, Moody started presenting the defense case by eliciting testimony from friends of the Hall family concerning the mental intellect of the defendant's relatives. He called Dr. E.M. Ingram, who testified to what he knew about Red Hall's uncles, one of whom he characterized as a "moron."

"How long have you considered him a moron?" Moody asked.

"Let's see," Dr. Ingram thought for a moment, "He's about forty-seven years old and since he was a child—he had an attack of typhoid pneumonia when he was six or seven years old. I treated him. He apparently got well, but afterwards, whenever I was around him, his mind didn't appear to have developed any more after that. I haven't seen him much since he became an adult, but he still acts that way."

"Do you know this boy here?" Moody asked, indicating the defendant.

"I do."

"Have you ever attended him or any of his people?"

"I attended his wife, Walcie, I believe it was on Christmas Day in 1941. I tended to her in confinement."

"Was he there at that time?"

"Yes, sir."

"Did you have occasion to examine him?"

"I didn't examine him, but he had some kind of convulsion about the time of the termination of his wife's labor. He was sitting on the sofa, and he just passed out on his face onto the floor. I couldn't get to him. He laid there and breathed a time or two and got up and turned around, and I saw his face twitch around his eyes. He sat down on the sofa and never said a word."

Robinson cross-examined.

"Dr. Ingram, the time you refer to was during the delivery of his child?"

"Yes, sir."

"It was a difficult situation?"

"Yes, sir."

"The child wouldn't come right, and you had considerable trouble there?"

"Yes, sir."

"There was considerable pain involved, of course?"

"That's right."

"The child was dead?"

"That's right."

During Dr. Ingram's testimony, Hall became visibly nervous and began to cry. By the end of the cross-examination, he was sobbing. The witness was then excused, and Moody called Willie Henderson to the stand.

"Do you know James Waybern Hall, his father, his mother, his sister?"

"Yes, sir."

When Moody asked about Red's sister, Lucy, Henderson portrayed her as "child-minded."

"How long have you known the defendant's uncle, his mother's brother?"

"Since I was seven or eight years old. He was grown when I was a lad of a boy."

"From your viewpoint and own knowledge, what mentality would you say he was?"

"He's not normal. I wouldn't carry on business transactions with him. No one else does. Say something about him doing something, and they say, 'Don't pay attention. He's crazy.'"

Robinson took over the questioning and attempted to dispel Moody's theory that a strain of mental defectiveness ran in Red's family. "Mr. Henderson, do you know anything about the long siege of pneumonia the uncle had when he was five or six years old?"

"I didn't know him when he was a child."

"You know nothing about the long spell of pneumonia he had at the time Dr. Ingram treated him?"

"No, sir."

"You know nothing about him being normal up until that time?"

"No, sir."

With very few objections from Robinson, six more witnesses took the stand to give their impressions of the mental condition of Hall and members of his family. A distant relative mentioned another one of Red's uncles who was too defective to serve in the army.

"He couldn't follow simple orders; he wouldn't fall in when the bugle sounded, and if he was marching, he wouldn't stop when they said, 'Halt!'"

According to a neighbor, the uncle "does things I don't think a normal person would do."

"Describe them," Moody asked the witness to explain further.

"One time, down in the field where we had rented land, he was standing there throwing rocks against a tree. A normal man, I don't think, would do that."

"Do you consider him sane or insane?"

"I don't know whether he's insane or not," the witness said. "I know he isn't right."

Robinson offered no objection to the layman's opinion.

When Moody called Walcie Hall to the stand, Red tried to smile at his former wife but started to cry again and continued to do so throughout much of her testimony. His lack of emotional control caused onlookers to murmur and whisper, distracting the court. Judge Auten brought the gavel down to stop the noise.

"This is a trial," he said, "And the jury has to hear. I'll have to ask the people in the gallery to be quiet or I'll instruct the bailiff to clear the courtroom."

Under Moody's sympathetic questioning, Walcie, now twenty-nine, recalled her life with Red and his penchant for rambling and sudden departures from home.

"Did he explain why he left?"

"No particular reason."

"Did he ask you for a divorce?"

"Yes, sir."

"You gave him a divorce?"

"Yes."

"At the time you were living with him, did you notice peculiarities about him?"

"Yes."

"What peculiarities did you notice?"

"He is what I call 'a double-minded person'—a mind to do good and another mind that conflicts with that."

"During a period of three years, we'll say, how many jobs do you think he had?"

"I guess six or eight."

"Was he fired from these places?"

"He just walked out most of the time."

"Did he give you any excuse for having walked out?"

"He said some jobs were too hard, some didn't pay enough, and the hours were too long in others. It didn't seem he was ever satisfied with anything he would do."

Robinson crossed, "He wasn't satisfied with the hours he worked and the pay, etc.?"

"That," Walcie nodded. "And it seemed his mind was disturbed all the time about something."

"Especially about working?"

"Yes, working, too."

When Walcie stepped down, the jury was left with a depiction of Hall as lazy instead of crazy.

Moody called his next witness. "State your name, please."

"Sam J. Hall. Elder Sam J. Hall."

The defendant searched his father's face but didn't see any etching of embarrassment over the shame that had befallen the family name. It was the same face Red had seen all his life, the face that had glared at him so often, the face that became distorted with malevolent hatred when the man whipped the boy. Remembering such abusive treatment, Red couldn't understand why the whimper that escaped from his lips was for the witness and not for himself, the accused.

"What is your occupation?" Moody asked.

"Farmer and Minister of the Gospel."

"How many children do you have?"

"We have ten children."

"This is your wife here?" indicating Eva Hall.

"Yes, sir."

"Your oldest son, what is his name?"

"Lawrence Hall."

"Where is he?"

"In Germany in the infantry, the last we heard of him."

"Who is the son nearest to him in age?"

"Three years younger than Lawrence. Gilmer Hall. The last we heard of him, he was in California. He left when he was seventeen years old. We heard from him in November 1936, and we've not heard from him since."

"You don't know where he is or whether he is living or dead?"

"No. My eldest son put on a search for him."

"Who's your next son?"

"James Waybern. We had a child born between Gil and Waybern that died at birth, and I have two sons younger than Waybern. And five daughters."

Then Moody concentrated on Lucy, who was described by her father as "of a weak mind. We watch her close. In her early life, she had fits occasionally. We have to keep her continually under the family's care. She never goes even to the nearest neighbor's place alone. We don't risk her to do cooking or anything by herself."

The senior Hall went on to label some members of his wife's family as mental incompetents, saying one of Red's uncles had been confined for a while in Fort Roots, a veterans' hospital in North Little Rock with facilities for alcoholics and the mentally ill.

Red was showing signs of strain, but his mood brightened considerably during the lunch recess, when Walcie brought in their baby boy. Bouncing the child on his knee, the proud father had forgotten something special, but Walcie reminded him.

"It's his birthday. He's two years old today."

"Oh, my goodness, that's right." Red started singing "Happy Birthday."

The baby was beyond the cooing and gurgling stage, but his mama still had to interpret most of his words. He didn't seem to recognize his father.

Court reconvened at 1:30 p.m. when Sam Hall continued his testimony.

"I ask you about your son, Waybern Hall," Moody said. "Has he any physical peculiarities?"

"Yes, sir, he demonstrated physical peculiarities all his life."

"He demonstrated mental peculiarities?"

"He was different from other children. Even at the age of six or seven, he would ramble all over the county, and it was difficult keeping up with him. At thirteen or fourteen, he began to go on long trips. Once, when he was fourteen, he sent us a card that said he was up above Topeka, Kansas. He made a trip every year and several trips a year ever since."

"You testified this morning that you're a minister of the Gospel and a farmer," Moody said. "To what church are you a minister?"

"We are Baptists. I've been exercising in a public way since 1926. I was ordained in 1930."

"I'll ask if you have a Christian home?"

"We try to maintain the home that way."

"Do you say prayers before meals?"

"That custom I have practiced all my married life. We often call in the neighbors and preach in the home."

"Did your boy participate in the prayers?"

"He didn't offer the prayers himself, but in the religious services he was very obedient there."

"He had been taught to say prayers before he ate?"

"That's the way he was brought up, yes sir."

"He had a religious, God-fearing home?"

"Yes, sir, we strive for that end."

Moody changed the subject. "How long have you known your mother-in-law?"

"Thirty-seven years, I believe. She lives near my home."

"What is her age?"

"She's eighty-one years old."

"During the period of time you've known her, comparing her with other people, do you consider her sane or insane?"

"She is considered insane."

"I object," Robinson said.

"Sustained."

"On what grounds, Your Honor? I'm showing family history."

"I don't see where that has any connection," Auten explained. "You're getting into collateral matter. You don't say whether it was an accident that brought it about or what."

The question was put to the witness. "Do you know of her having an accident that affected her mind?"

"No, sir."

"What did Dr. Ingram advise?"

"He asked would my wife be willing for her mother to be placed in a nervous hospital owing to the fact that she was by herself. Her husband died some thirty years ago."

"Dr. Ingram asked you to place her in the insane asylum?"

"He asked would my wife be willing for that to be done, but she objected."

Moody asked about Red's uncle who hadn't performed well in the army.

"I gave testimony concerning his condition and mind to the draft board."

"Now, do you recall any accident your son, Waybern Hall, ever sustained?"

"Nothing of a very serious nature." But Hall went on to narrate his version of Red's childhood accident, implying that it had been the boy's own fault for letting a pole slip and hit himself. After his testimony, Samuel Hall stepped down from the stand, his posture as straight as the path he professed to walk.

During the final day of the trial, Conway auto dealer Earl Parks told Faulkner County sheriff Woodruff that he and his wife had come close to witnessing, unknowingly, the murder of J.D. Newcomb Jr. by Red Hall. Mr. and Mrs. Parks had just finished eating lunch at their home and were on their way to Parks's office in Conway when they observed two men scuffling. Parks slowed to stop, but his wife urged him to drive away. She thought the commotion was only a fight between two drunks. Her husband agreed and drove on. Mrs. Parks said that as they reached the intersection of US 64 and US 65, the car in which the two men had been struggling passed them, but they saw only the driver, who stopped and looked at the highway signs before proceeding north on 65. The couple, who also operated a gas station at their home, read about Hall's arrest but said nothing to anyone about the incident because they were afraid that he might escape from custody and kill them. Mr. Parks thought he had seen Hall previously, and Mrs. Parks said that either on the day of his arrest or the preceding day, Hall drove up to their filling station in a taxicab, but several customers were in the place, and he drove away without saying anything. Hall was never asked about this.

The defense called their next witness, Dr. R.F. Darnall, who recited his impressive medical credentials, including forty-eight years as a psychiatrist.

Stone Creek Bridge, south of Conway, where Hall killed J.D. Newcomb Jr. *Photo by Wyatt Jones.*

"Dr. Darnall," Moody began, "Can you tell me what a psychopathic personality is?"

"The term psychopath is composed of two words which mean mind and disease. It means a diseased mind. That is the literal translation of what it means; a man or woman with a diseased mind."

"There are varying stages of psychopathic personalities, aren't there?"

"It is pretty difficult to explain without going into detail. The idea that a man could not be psychopathic without being insane is wrong. Thousands of people mentally sick and not insane are walking the streets today. The men or women who are insane to such an extent as to be dangerous to themselves or personal property of other people are those who are deprived of their liberty. There are many thousands of people who are mentally sick and not legally insane; that is the reason we call them psychopaths. They are sick but not legally insane. They have not had an episode of misconduct that brings them in conflict with the law. Many times it is their environment and the fact that they get along without much friction, then something happens out of the ordinary where it requires an unusual amount of restraint of which they are found wanting. A whole chain is only as strong as its weakest link; and so it is with a mentally sick person. They get along, many of them, three score years and ten, with

112

little peculiar eccentricities. Stress has not been offered to bring about the break. That is my observation of psychopathic people."

"In other words, Doctor, a psychopathic personality is—what you say—not legally insane because he hasn't performed any act to cause him to be legally insane."

"No. The truth is that in his allotted years, nothing has happened that he couldn't take care of, but the stage is all set. Certain things in his makeup are wanting, but he doesn't show that sometimes. Those people are really the most dangerous because they are looked on as being ordinary folks. It is just because the exacting moment has not been put on them."

"In other words, it hasn't hit the weak link in the chain?"

"The application is true of people who are physically sick. Thousands of people are physically ill who are not in a hospital, and they roll along not knowing they're sick until something happens. There is nothing mysterious about mental sickness any more than physical."

"If the chain breaks then he is legally insane?"

"I object," Robinson said.

"The law permits him to be—" Darnall started to answer, but Auten cut him off.

"Objection sustained. At the proper time, the court will instruct the jury what legal insanity is."

"Doctor," Moody continued, "A person with a psychopathic personality, what reaction does he have toward the feeling of people around him?"

"That depends on his makeup. There are no two people alike. Some get along very well until they develop the feeling that they are not being treated right. They develop ideas of persecution. They feel they are not evening the score with someone. That individual may have started out all right, only a condition arose which he could not meet. Some of the most dangerous people are out in the open, enjoying liberty and are psychopathic."

On cross-examination, Robinson asked, "I believe you say that there are thousands of people with what is spoken of in medical terms as a psychopathic personality who are not insane?"

"As I understand the law, it says that when the mental condition of a person is such that he becomes dangerous to himself, other people, or personal property of other people, then he may be insane."

"But thousands of people are not insane?"

"They have not been so declared, no."

Darnall was then excused, and Dr. R.E. Rowland was sworn in.

"Doctor," Moody began, "Have you examined this boy, Waybern Hall?"

"Yes, sir, I examined him last night."

"Who was with you?"

"Dr. Brown."

"Have you interviewed the father as to the history of this boy?"

"Yes, sir."

"The mother as to the history of the boy?"

"Some, yes, sir."

"What are your findings?"

"We note that he has a bad family history. His maternal grandmother is defective. His sister, Lucy, is a developmental defect who suffers with a neurosis and requires continual care. He has a brother who hasn't been heard from for years. He has an uncle who is a former patient at Fort Roots—making probably three or four in the immediate family who are defective. He was normal as a child, probably. He had typhoid fever and later sustained a head injury. Following that, he has had a peculiar life. From a physical standpoint, he is able-bodied and normal in stature, but he shows a peculiar atrophic change on the outer side of his right leg and a patch on the left leg in which some neurological disturbance has caused the hairs to turn grey in those spots."

"That mental condition caused the hairs on the leg to be colored?"

"The hair has turned gray on these particular spots, showing it was an organic thing."

"Did you find any other symptoms suggesting to you his mental deficiency other than what you have testified?"

"Not physically."

"In your conversation with him, did you discover any other mental disturbances he may have?"

"From the history left at the State Hospital and from my examination, I would say that he is a psychopathic personality. With the periods of unconsciousness and the episodes he has had, his urge to move about from place to place—tramping, we call it. He was a tramp at the age of fourteen."

"Is that a psychopathic personality?"

"Yes. And I suppose you want me to define psychopathic personality?"

"I do."

"It is a person either born or reduced from disease or defect who hasn't got the inhibitory forces. He doesn't profit by experience. He is easily influenced and follows the lines of least resistance. He hasn't a normal mind of his own."

"Does a psychopath have a mind that can determine what is right and what is wrong?"

"He does not. He is wobbly and emotionally unstable. Psychopathic personalities are customarily egotistical, self-centered, and play to the galleries."

"In other words, he wants the spotlight on him?"

"That's right. He is very apt to brag."

Moody turned the witness over to opposing counsel.

"Just a whole lot of people like that, isn't there, Doctor?" Robinson said.

"Yes, sir."

"Doctor, the first part of your testimony in relation to the family history is all hearsay on your part?"

"It is. Yes, sir."

"In the nature of a hypothetical question propounded to yourself?"

"Yes, sir."

"Otherwise, you assumed those things to be true?"

"Yes, sir."

"For instance, you assumed to be true that there was something wrong with the mentality of the defendant's grandmother?"

"Yes, sir."

"You assumed it was true that something was wrong with the mentality of two of his uncles?"

"Yes, sir."

"In order for that part of your testimony to have any weight at all, those things that you assume to be true, would actually have to be true?"

"Yes, sir."

"If they're not true, then that part of your testimony carries no weight."

"That's correct."

"With reference to the physical findings, I believe you said you found some discoloration of the hair on his leg?"

"Yes, sir."

"That it was due to some nervous change?"

"Due to an atrophic change."

"As a matter of fact, it is generally due to an injury, isn't it?"

"Well, yes sir."

"You even see that in stock. Horses that had a sore on their back, the hair turns white?"

"Yes, sir."

After Robinson had finished questioning Rowland, Moody delved deeper during redirect.

"You examined this boy?"

"Yes, sir."

"What did you find from your examination as an expert?"

Robinson objected. "He has already been questioned once about that, and may it please the court, he went over it thoroughly."

"Go ahead," Auten said to Moody. "When you do ask the question, I'll permit the State to cross-examine further."

"What did you find on your examination?" Moody asked Dr. Rowland, but Auten sought to avoid just a reiteration of already stated opinions.

"He told about finding the white hairs," the judge said and then quizzed the witness himself. "Is there anything additional you haven't testified about already?"

"Yes, sir. The further examination last night."

"State what you found on your examination."

"On observation, he gave a history of vague hallucinations. He heard voices and was able to designate one voice as the voice of a cousin, and he answered that cousin. He was emotionless. He is out of tune with his environment. I believe this had an early onset. Getting back to sanity, he probably knows the difference between right and wrong and probably knows the consequences of his acts, but by reason of his inability to profit by experience and by reason of his lack of inhibitory forces, I don't believe he should be held accountable."

"In making this examination, you say the color of the hairs on one of his legs is caused from a nervous condition?" Moody asked.

"Yes, sir."

"Did you find in your examination any scars from any injury to his leg?"

"No, sir."

"If a scar had been there over a period of years, you would have found some scar tissue?"

"I think I would have."

Though Moody was finished with the witness, Robinson wasn't.

"There are many injuries that do not necessarily leave scars?" the prosecutor asked.

"Yes, sir."

"Isn't your opinion based on hypothetical questions propounded to you?"

"Yes, sir."

"You are assuming other things?"

"Yes, sir."

"You say he failed to profit by experience?"

"Yes, sir."

"What experience did he fail to profit by?"

"All of his experiences."

"What experience had he had?"

"Every time he violated the law or failed to follow his father's instructions."

"I want to know what experience he had that he failed to profit by," Robinson bristled with exasperation. "On the contrary, hasn't he profited by all his experiences?"

"On a minor scale, though."

"You say he has vague hallucinations?"

"Yes, sir."

"That is what he tells *you*." Robinson's sarcasm wasn't lost on the spectators.

Members of the jury were taking their job seriously, or at least it looked that way. Straight-faced from the start, they paid attention and hadn't seemed to be sleepy or bored even through the clinical psychiatric verbiage.

Moody called the next witness, another psychiatrist, Dr. L.R. Brown, who had spent only two and a half hours interviewing Hall the previous night but had determined Hall was psychotic.

"He explained he has been having hallucinations for three or four years, and he complains of fainting or falling-out spells—suggestive of an epileptic equivalent—in which he loses consciousness, and at times he has light tremors of the arms, hands, and feet, and he has symptoms of a schizophrenic condition." Brown drew an analogy between the workings of the defendant's mind and those of a cab Hall might have driven. "The steering gear is badly out of line."

"Would you say he is sane or insane?"

"Insane."

Under cross-examination, Brown admitted his time with Hall had been meager and didn't allow for the "better tests" that he customarily administered in his practice. When Brown said he had drawn most of his conclusions from Dr. Kolb's report and from newspaper accounts, given that this was hearsay testimony, much of it was stricken from the record.

It wasn't exactly the note he wished to close on, but Moody had run out of witnesses.

"Your Honor, the defense rests."

After a brief recess, during the state's rebuttal testimony, eleven people who had known Red Hall at various times in his life said they believed he was sane.

Dr. N.T. Hollis, a member of the staff at the State Hospital, said he and six colleagues were in unanimous agreement with Kolb's findings that Hall was sane and responsible. Robinson tried to simplify terms used by the psychiatrists and asked Hollis to define psychopathic personality one more time.

"That is a term even our authorities in psychiatric work don't agree on," Hollis said. "It's just a minor classification. It has nothing to do with psychosis. Psychosis means a man is insane. Without psychosis means he is sane. Having a psychopathic personality has nothing to do with sanity."

"He can have a psychopathic personality and not be insane?"

"Yes, sir.

"The same way a person might have black hair and not be insane."

"That is correct."

"I have nothing further for this witness, Your Honor," Robinson said.

Moody continued the weird turn the questioning had taken.

"Mr. Robinson asked you if a person with black hair could have a psychosis. Could a person with red hair have a psychosis?"

"Yes, sir."

The jury looked at Hall with his handsome head of red hair, but their faces gave no hint as to their thoughts.

"That's all," Moody said.

As Hollis stepped down, Robinson called Dr. Kolb to the stand again, and the doctor complied with Robinson's request to read from a logbook that contained details of Hall's behavior after he had been sent to the state Hospital for observation. Kolb's notes were meticulous with down-to-the-minute comings and goings between the jail and the hospital. He also presented findings from thorough physical examinations: X-rays, spinal fluid tests, neurological functions, pupillary reflexes, muscular reflexes and so forth. All were normal. Hall hadn't told Kolb about any hallucinations.

When Moody cross-examined, he finally allowed Kolb to explain why he had insisted Hall be returned to the jail every evening.

"That was based on an experience recently where a man was sent from the penitentiary to the hospital for a mental examination. I was warned he was dangerous and might escape. I asked for a guard, and one was provided, but the man escaped anyway and went to Texarkana and killed a man and is now serving a life sentence in Texas."

Moody returned to the subject of psychopathic personalities, but even he seemed to be tiring of the topic. The spectators certainly were. Some were stirring restlessly, and one yawned loudly as if he were in the comfort of his own home. Moody got the message, and the witness was dismissed.

"That's the State's case," Robinson said, "May it please the Court."

10

"THE BOY'S CRAZY"

The day had been a long one and still wasn't over, but Judge Auten called for a thirty-minute recess. Meals were brought to the jurors, and spectators dispersed to nearby restaurants and cafés, making quick work of their suppers so as not to lose their courtroom seats.

The night session opened with a brief closing argument by Chief Deputy Prosecutor Otis T. Nixon filling in for a tardy Sam Robinson.

"Who's he?" Hall asked Moody.

"That's Robinson's associate," Moody told his client. "Don't worry. After he gets through, it'll be our turn at the jury."

"All the evidence presented by the State has gone undisputed," Nixon said. "This is the most perfect case of circumstantial evidence ever heard in the Pulaski Circuit Court. And the defendant made a confession in front of one of the best police reporters in Arkansas."

Moody objected. "Yes, I agree with you, Mr. Nixon, that beautiful Joe Wirges is a newspaperman, but that hasn't anything to do with this case."

Judge Auten ruled, "Mr. Wirges was a witness in the case and that can be stated."

Nixon continued. "Hall is a cold, calculating individual; cruel, brutal, and unrepentant. Please see that he gets what he deserves, and what he deserves is death."

As Nixon sat down, Moody arose and approached the panel. During his forty-minute summation, he tried to plant the seed of reasonable doubt in the jurors' minds: "The State has failed utterly in presenting a case. There has been no proof that a murder has been committed. The skeleton shown here has not been convincingly identified as that of Mrs. Hall. It is most unusual about this corpus delicti. In fact, it's a tailor-made corpus delicti. One man found a bone here, another found one somewhere else, and before long, they had gathered up what they brought here and asked you to believe these are the remains of Mrs. Hall. Then they found this idiot," Moody flicked his wrist toward Hall. "And he readily told them he had committed a murder. The boy's crazy. If you gentlemen convict him, it will only be because he is mentally sick, and that is no crime."

Sam Robinson had returned to the courtroom and presented the state's rebuttal, first mentioning motive again.

"Hall killed his wife after she had threatened to leave him, and he was afraid she would tell what she knew about the trip to Oregon. He killed her to shut her up forever."

And then the prosecutor addressed the issue of insanity, saying, "He's not crazy. He demonstrated that when he took her to that lonely spot, where he thought the body would never be found. A crazy man would not wait and look for a secluded spot. He'd murder in the presence of witnesses. Hall is far from crazy, and I'm convinced you gentlemen of the jury will do your sworn duty and return a verdict that will carry the death penalty."

Judge Auten followed summations with instructions for the jury with the caveat that the burden of proof was on the prosecution: "The mere fact that the defendant was charged with a crime raises no presumption that he is guilty. And under the law, the defendant is not required to take the stand as a witness in his own behalf; you are not to consider his failure to testify in arriving at your verdict. You shall not permit any sympathy, prejudice, or bias to influence or affect your consideration. If you are convinced by a preponderance of evidence and to a moral certainty that the defendant is guilty, it is your duty to convict him. Now, first degree murder means that the act was committed with premeditation and malice aforethought. In coming to your decision on that point, you are to use reason and common sense. Gentlemen of the jury, you have four possible verdicts:

Guilty of first-degree murder without recommendation of clemency, which means the penalty is automatically fixed by law at death.

Guilty of first-degree murder with a recommendation for clemency, which would mean a sentence of life imprisonment.

Not guilty.

Not guilty by reason of insanity, in which case Mr. Hall would be confined to the State Hospital until pronounced sane."

The court clerk gave the foreman a slip of paper on which the verdict would be written, and at that point, Red Hall's life was put in the hands of twelve people he didn't know. He looked at their faces as they stood to file out of the courtroom. Some looked back at him. For once, he knew a smile would get him nothing, but he smiled anyway out of habit.

Deliberations began at 11:15 p.m., and only forty minutes later, a rap on the door of the jury room signaled a verdict had been reached, and five minutes after that, all interested parties were back in the courtroom to hear what Red Hall's fate would be. His parents sat on either side of him. His mother's eyes had a haunted look, as if she were already lamenting the loss of her son. She held a handkerchief with a dainty design of violets on it. She kept it close to her face, trying to smother the anguish that would follow her like a shadow until her own death.

Though the night session had lasted past midnight, the audience was still sizeable, and Judge Auten warned them that he would not tolerate any demonstrations.

"Has the jury reached a verdict?" he asked.

"We have, Your Honor," replied Mr. Cooke, the foreman.

The judge directed the clerk to hand him the paper with the written verdict and, after reading it, gave it back to the clerk, who passed it on to the foreman.

"Will the defendant please rise?" Auten said, and Hall stood up with his attorney. Everyone's attention focused on Cooke. "Mr. Foreman, in the matter of the State versus James Waybern Hall, how do you find?"

"We find the defendant guilty," Cooke said.

A loud gasp came from someone in the gallery.

"Do you recommend clemency?" Auten asked the foreman.

"We do not."

If the spectators were expecting tears or other signs of self-pity from Red, they were sorely disappointed. He was as apathetic about his own doom as he had been about his victims'. His father, stoic throughout the trial, remained so, but Red's mother shuddered and began to cry softly.

"Mr. Hall," Auten said, "Do you know of any legal reason why you should not be sentenced to death?"

Red was silent for a moment before saying, "I sure do."

"And what is that reason?"

"Insanity."

"The jury has decided you are sane. Do you have any other reason?"

"Yes, I do. I'm not guilty."

"Well, the jury has decided otherwise," Auten said and thanked the twelve men for their service. "Because of the late hour," he added, "Sentencing will be set at a future date. Court is adjourned." And the gavel came down.

A deputy quickly snapped some handcuffs on Red and whisked him off to the county jail.

The next day, a lot of newspaper readers learned a new word when they read a headline about the trial's outcome: "Jury Declares James W. Hall Slew His Wife—Decrees Death for Uxoricide."

At the same time that justice was putting the whammy on Red Hall, Arkansas was celebrating the homecoming of Captain Corydon McAlmont Wassell, a Little Rock physician turned war hero. The naval officer had won national acclaim for his courageous rescue of wounded soldiers from Java during the war. Before arriving in Little Rock, he visited the naval ordnance plant at Camden, the same plant where E.C. Adams would have been working if he hadn't crossed paths with Red Hall.

Even though Red's trial was over, the public's interest in him wasn't. He made such good copy, newspaper subscriptions had increased dramatically since his arrest. This was especially true at the *Log Cabin Democrat*, the newspaper in Faulkner County. A relative of Hall's who said she hadn't seen him since he was a small boy bought a subscription so she could keep up with the case.

She said the youth was "a mean little boy," but his parents were "fine people."

Many detective magazines and comic books of the era contained writings about Hall. They went for the sensationalist factor and gave him lurid monikers to hook the readers: the "Arkansas Butcher," the "Kill-Crazy Murderer of Little Rock" and the "Dr. Jekyll of Arkansas." The allusion to Robert Louis Stevenson's story about a man with two very different temperaments might have referred to Hall more appropriately as the evil personification of "Mr. Hyde."

But it was the *Gazette*'s Joe Wirges who was the main conduit through which the public really came to know Red Hall. When Wirges visited him in the county jail the day after his trial ended, Hall looked dazed.

"I'm glad you agreed to see me," Wirges said. "I wasn't sure you would, after I testified against you."

"No hard feelings."

"How are you holding up?"

"I'm a little depressed, Mr. Wirges, but not about the verdict. It's this solitary confinement. I've asked the jailer to transfer me to the upper floor with the other prisoners, but the sheriff has ordered him to keep me by myself. Another few days in here alone, and I'll need no examination for sanity. How long do you think the appeal will take?"

"I don't know, but you won't have to stay here while you wait." Wirges told him. "They'll be transferring you to Tucker as soon as you're sentenced."

"Oh, OK." Red was relieved, even though Wirges was referring to the death house.

"Did the verdict surprise you?"

"It did," Red admitted. "Then again, you never know what a jury will do. I'll tell you one thing, though. These last three days have worn me out. I got awfully tired of sitting in one place so long, my butt went to sleep. And I've had a constant headache for a week. As for the trial, I can't complain about anything. My lawyer turned in a swell job, but that Mr. Robinson sure can talk."

"Show me a lawyer who can't," Wirges said.

Red laughed.

"Do you think the judgment was fair?" Wirges asked.

"Honestly, I believe they should have committed me to the State Hospital. I know I'm not sane. There's something wrong with my power of reasoning, but with proper treatment, I probably could have recovered in a year's time."

"Are you afraid, Red?"

"No, I don't fear death, but I'm not looking forward to the dying part."

On May 14, 1945, Judge Auten officially sentenced Hall to die in the electric chair. His date with "old Sparky" was set at "the twenty-ninth day of June between the hours of sunrise and sunset." The sentence, however, was stayed when M.V. Moody filed an appeal to the Arkansas State Supreme Court. He raised four points: first, the confession was coerced and, therefore inadmissible; second, that the defendant was insane; third, that the state failed to prove the corpus delicti; and finally, that the defendant's confession to Dr. Kolb fell under doctor/patient privilege. The court wasn't expected to rule until after the justices' summer vacation.

Red was optimistic about the appeal, saying, "I don't believe I'll be electrocuted."

The day after sentencing, Detectives Peterson and Judd talked to Hall as he awaited transfer to prison. Wirges was there and would be driving down to Tucker to cover Red going through the prison gates. The lawmen and reporter had spent so much time with Red, he had come to consider them almost friends, his accusations of coercion forgotten, and so his departure for prison wasn't as gloomy as one might think. His companions made it a lot easier on him.

"Red, we thought about having Joe drive you down by himself, but we tried that once," Peterson said. "Didn't we, Joe?"

"I don't know what you're talking about," Wirges said.

"See, Red," Peterson explained. "There was a woman who had murdered somebody, and Joe went down to write about her going to prison, just like he's doing with you today. Would have made a good news story, but when they got to the pen, the warden wouldn't take her, said nobody had told him about it and he wasn't taking any woman. The deputy who had escorted her threw up his hands and said he'd done his part, and he went back to Little Rock. Well, Joe wanted a scoop for the *Gazette*, so he stalled until the *Democrat* had already gone to press. He drove the woman around for a while and talked to her, and then he put her on a train. She never served a day."

"Naw, you're wolfin' me." Red laughed. "Did you really do that, Mr. Wirges?"

"That's how the story goes," Joe said.

"Are you going to eat with Red when it comes time for his last meal?" Judd asked Wirges.

"I usually do."

"Really?" Red asked.

"If you don't mind," Wirges said.

"I'd be honored."

Sheriff Caple and Deputies Farmer and Shelton arrived to deliver Red to death row at Tucker. As they rode through various small towns en route to the prison, Hall would point out places where he had hitched rides.

"If the people who picked me up then had known of the reputation that I was going to get later, they would have been mighty scared, wouldn't they?"

At Tucker, Red went through the intake process just like any other convict, and notes state that he had on his person a total of seventy cents. Other inmates hailed him as a celebrity and wished him well, to which he boasted, "Guys, they threw the book at me, but I can take it."

In October, the High Court affirmed the lower court's judgment and the sentence of death. A month later, the court denied a rehearing, and the new execution date was set for January 4, 1946. Hall had only one more chance, and that was clemency from Arkansas governor Ben Laney. The governor's diary, which looks more like an appointment book, is now a part of public records at the University of Central Arkansas's Torreyson Library in Conway. It has an entry for Friday, November 16, 1945, that simply reads, "9:15 a.m. Mrs. Ingram," presumably referring to one of Red's in-laws on his mother's side of the family, maybe even his mother herself. It isn't clear if the meeting took place, but two days before the scheduled execution, Hall's parents and his brother Lawrence (recently discharged from the army) pleaded for mercy, contending that Hall was mentally deranged. M.V. Moody also tried a last-minute intervention but to no avail. And then Hall himself wrote a letter to the state's executive, saying, "I am not guilty of everything I am accused of." But Laney said, "No evidence to justify extension of clemency has been brought out in appeals."

An anonymous woman mailed a letter to the FBI in care of the governor's office. In the correspondence, she claimed to be Hall's lover and that she had murdered Fayrene. The envelope's postmark was Paragould, Arkansas. A lady from Augusta sent a letter to Laney's office, begging for a postponement of the execution until Hall's "soul could be saved. He is a poor misfortunate sinner without money or friends to help him." Laney's secretary, W.J. Smith, said the letter to the FBI would be kept, but the other one wouldn't be included in the file.

Sometime after Hall went to the death house, he alleged that two former convicts had committed the hitchhike murders and gave officers their names, saying he had been covering up for the two, expecting them to come to his rescue. He didn't press the issue when nobody believed him.

The end of World War II had brought peace but also left a lot of fallout to be tidied up. One such unresolved bit of business concerned an American-born man named William Joyce. Raised in Ireland, Joyce was an informant for the British in the Irish War for Independence. After the Anglo-Irish Treaty of 1921, his family moved to England, where his Fascist ideology took hold. Hitler's writings and speeches further radicalized Joyce, and he immigrated to Germany, where he became a radio propagandist personality known as Lord Haw Haw, the European equivalent of Tokyo Rose. The British convicted him of treason and hanged him exactly one day before Red Hall's execution date.

After weeks of extreme anxiety bordering on a nervous breakdown, Red had grown calm and resigned to die.

"We were surprised to find he had a change of heart," Assistant Superintendent Henslee told reporters the night before the execution. "We found him feeling fine and happy. He carried on a jocular conversation while the barber was shaving his head. I told him about other prisoners betting on whether Governor Laney would grant a reprieve. He counted his money and said, 'I've got a little more than six dollars that I'm ready to bet that I *will* get a stay. I wish one of you would let the boys know. I'm sure I'd find a taker, but I still believe he'd lose.'"

Prison regulations thwarted his desire to gamble on his life.

Red's last day on Earth was busy. He spoke with several visitors. Some of it was just small talk. His brother told him Faulkner County was having a flu epidemic.

"Nearly everybody has had it," Lawrence said.

"I sure hope you're not giving it to me," Red playfully jabbed his brother through the bars.

Besides his family, he entertained out-of-state lawmen who were still trying to attribute unsolved murders to him. Lawmen from Kansas again attempted to tie him to the Lambert/Nipper slayings. Captain Scroggin accompanied the officers, and they spent a considerable amount of time with the condemned man. He conceded that he had been in the vicinity of the murders the day they occurred but steadfastly denied any knowledge of the double homicide.

Police Chief Jake Sims from Seminole, Oklahoma, who had interviewed Hall on numerous occasions, telephoned one last time about the James Owen slaying, but Red was confessing no more.

Another request that couldn't be fulfilled was Red's choice of dessert for his last meal. He asked for fresh strawberries, but it was impossible to find any out of season, so he opted for strawberry ice cream. The rest of his supper included a big steak and pork chops with trimmings. He called it a feast and enjoyed it very much. As promised, he shared the meal with Joe Wirges.

"Have you ever thought of donating your body to science?" Wirges asked him.

"No, but that's not a bad idea. Maybe they could figure out what's wrong with me, why I did what I did."

"You could donate your corneas to a blind person."

"My what?"

"Your eyes."

Red stuttered in disbelief. "You—you mean they can take a dead man's eyes and put them in somebody else?"

"Yeah, you could help somebody see again."

"That would be great." Red was enthusiastic about the suggestion. "I'll tell Mr. Henslee to give my eyes to a soldier boy."

The night before Hall's execution, a blanket of fog covered most of Arkansas. Five people were killed in car wrecks across the state.

January 4, 1946. 6:45 a.m. It was that peaceful time just before dawn when yawning sleepyheads mosey to the kitchen for the first cup of coffee that will ease them into their daily routine. But a flurry of activity was taking place at Tucker Prison. Superintendent Tom Cogdill and Assistant Henslee permitted A.Z. Clemmons, several ministers and Joe Wirges to go to Red's cell. They gathered at the bars, where they found him in good spirits and smiling. He wore an improvised nightcap to hide his bald head; he had asked authorities to give a lock of his hair to his mother. The pastors read a few Scriptures, and those so inclined joined in prayer. Clemmons bowed his head, too. As the men of God completed their task and prepared to leave, Hall spoke.

"I have no ill feeling toward any man. The men who sent me here to die performed their duty as they saw it, and I can't be resentful toward them. I hold no grudge against anyone."

Clemmons stepped up closer to the bars and accepted Red's proffered hand.

"James, why did you kill our daughter?" Clemmons asked.

"Mr. Clemmons, I'm telling you the truth. It was an accident. You know I loved Fayrene. I was crazy about her. It all happened as we were leaving that dance hall. We had an argument and slapped each other. I took her home and when we got there, I learned she was dead. I'm telling you the truth. It was an accident."

Ignoring the lie, Clemmons said, "If you had only brought her home to us, or at least told us where you hid the body. We could have given our little girl a decent Christian burial."

"I was afraid," Hall said. "I didn't know what I was doing."

Clemmons paused a moment and then continued: "May God have mercy on you. I can't. But I hold no ill will toward your folks, James."

"Thank you." Hall said.

After the guests departed, preparations for the execution moved forward, including the reading of the death warrant by the warden.

The electric chair awaiting Red had been in service since 1913, when the state legislature abolished hanging and designated electrocution as the method of capital punishment. A professor from the University of Arkansas built Ol' Sparky for about $1,000. Prison officials were apprehensive about the chair's efficiency, so they tested it by electrocuting a cow. How exactly this was done is not clear. The apparatus, made of sturdy oak, was first used on a man named Lee Simms on September 5, 1913, at the former Arkansas Penitentiary (nicknamed "the Walls"), located on a fifteen-acre plot of land southwest of Little Rock. The prison's electrician conducted the execution of Simms, said the *Arkansas Gazette*, "without delay and without producing convulsions or twitching in the unconscious form such as make hangings horrible." One unfortunate person was executed twice in 1923 when it was discovered he was still breathing as he was being put into a coffin. The visibly shaken warden ordered him put back in the chair and electrocuted again.

Red Hall's execution was on many people's social calendars. Witnesses began congregating in the prison office long before dawn, but officials limited admittance to sixty-four people, mostly peace officers and newspaper correspondents. Clemmons was also present. Fifteen people, including two women, were denied entrance to the death house. Corrections officials challenged everyone's identity at the main gate. In addition to prison personnel, the Arkansas State Police had a high profile at all executions.

A white curtain obscured the view of witnesses as Hall entered the death chamber and walked to the chair without faltering. Guards worked in practiced unison to secure straps around his wrists and ankles and across his chest, and another corrections officer placed a brine-soaked felt electrode, like a metal skullcap, atop his shaved head. Another piece of wet felt went on his left ankle, and a black leather mask came down over his face. At 7:15 a.m., the curtain was drawn back, and a moment later, a flipped switch sent a sizzling electrical current through his body. Seven minutes later, the prison doctor pronounced him dead. Red Hall had hitched his last ride.

Then came a custom peculiar to the state of Arkansas. It had been the habit for many years to make a death mask of the newly deceased, the mold composed of plaster of Paris and then a layer of papier-mâché to make it more durable. Red Hall joined the rogue's gallery of men who had died in the electric chair, their death masks displayed in a large room at State Police Headquarters. When headquarters were moved to a new location in 1981, the masks were stored away. And then most of them disappeared. Someone knows what happened to them, but Someone isn't talking. Today, only two of the masks remain, and one is Red Hall's. His likeness, warehoused at the Old State House Museum in Little Rock, is mounted on wood with a metal plaque that reads: "James Waybern Hall, Age 24, Arkansas' Multiple Hitch-Hike Murderer, Electrocuted January 4, 1946 at Tucker Prison, Tucker, Arkansas." Some time ago, the mask fell to the floor, breaking off part of the forehead, but it was patched with wax. The two thousand volts of electricity that had jolted him from this world into the next caused his face to contort in a grimace, but looking at the mask, he appears to be smiling into eternity. The macabre practice of making such memento mori ended when Winthrop Rockefeller became governor in 1967.

Some of Arkansas's executed convicts, their bodies unwanted by their families, are buried on prison property, but Red Hall's family claimed his

Right: Hall's death mask made immediately after his execution. *Photo by the author.*

Below: James Waybern Hall's final resting place in Marcus Hill Cemetery. *Photo by the author.*

body, and McNutt Funeral Home in Conway took him back to Faulkner County. At midafternoon on the Saturday after the execution, Reverend W.D. Bowman, pastor of Rose City Baptist Church, officiated at Red's graveside service held at Marcus Hill Cemetery next to Marcus Hill Church. The casket was covered with light gray velour. Being January, flowers were not in abundance, but someone had managed to gather a few homegrown crimson camellias to decorate the grave. About thirty to forty people were in attendance; some were relatives and friends of relatives, but a few were there out of curiosity. Walcie paid her respects to the father of her child, but she showed little emotion. The ceremony was brief, and the mourners were quiet as they made their way back down the dusty lane. Today, the dirt road has been replaced by a paved one, and Marcus Hill Church is modernized, but the surrounding land looks much like it did in 1946. Trees rustle with the whispers of restless spirits as visitors contemplate the lives of those who lie buried there. James Waybern Hall's grave is marked by an inconspicuous flat stone that pays tribute to his service in the navy. His father requested the marker a few months after the execution. His parents don't share the same cemetery with him, but Walcie McKey is separated from Red by only one grave, her mother's. A tiny, unlettered tombstone is on the other side of Walcie, most likely the resting place of the infant who died moments after his birth in 1941.

11

ONE IN A LONG LINE
OF MONSTERS

S everal of the law officers who suspected Red Hall of killing people in their states would never have the definitive answers they had worked so hard to uncover. It was certainly true that Red made an awfully good candidate as the murderer in some of the cases.

"Closer to twenty-four," he had said.

Well, now, let's see. Here is a list of victims and possible victims:

The Black woman on North Santa Fe Avenue in Salina, Kansas, in 1938. Red claimed her as his first kill.

Ten Mexican migrant farm workers on the George Shoemaker ranch in Arizona in 1938. Red confessed to those.

Fayrene Clemmons Hall, Carl Hamilton, E.C. Adams, Doyle Mulherin and J.D. Newcomb Jr. Evidence corroborated Red's declarations of guilt in those cases.

He also said he killed an unnamed man (possibly a Bible salesman) in San Marcos, Texas, in December 1944. If Dallas detective Chief Fritz checked this out, no records can be found to substantiate Red's confession. W.M. Wren, sheriff of Hays County, of which San Marcos was the county seat, wired the *Arkansas Democrat* that he had no information on any slaying there at that time.

Dr. Merrill E. Lambert and Corporal Charles W. Nipper III in Kansas, October 1944. There's a good chance that Hall did kill these two men. He admitted to being in the vicinity when the murders were committed, and according to Nipper's cousin Bill Cook, no one else was ever charged with the murders. Nipper's parents, Charles Cotesworth Nipper and Minnie Nipper, owned a grocery store in Belmont, North Carolina. "Aunt Minnie talked quite a bit about the murder," Cook told Kevin Ellis with the *Gaston Gazette* in May 2016. "They suspected a serial killer, but that's all we ever knew." The corporal's father committed suicide in 1954, and Minnie sold the store soon afterward. She died in 1998, both parents going to their graves without knowing if their son's killer was ever brought to justice. The manner of death in the double homicide did fit Hall's modus operandi.

James Owen, Seminole, Oklahoma, December 1940. Hall told Joe Wirges he had been "a good boy" from 1939 until 1943, when he was married to Walcie. If he was telling the truth for once, he couldn't have killed James Owen in December 1940. But he strayed from home frequently during those years, sending back postcards from other states. And even though Owen hadn't picked up a hitchhiker, he was parked near a railroad track, so Red could have committed the murder, taken Owen's fifty dollars and then hopped a freight and arrived home in time for Christmas. Who is to be believed? Red? Or Seminole police chief Jake Sims, who had seen Red in Seminole on many occasions and said, "He has told us enough about it to convince us that he probably was the one."

Of the four hitchhike-related murders committed in and around Miami, Oklahoma, officials publicly named only one of the victims when they questioned Hall, Wehman J. Peacock Jr. It's possible that Hall killed Peacock, who went missing September 1, 1944, and presumably died then. Two weeks before that, Red and Fay were moving into W.A. Woods's apartment, and two weeks after Peacock's disappearance, Red killed Fay. We can't account for the time in between. Red could have taken off on a lark and murdered Peacock. Fay may even have found out about it, giving Red another reason to silence her. The idea that the killer had exchanged clothes with the victim, however, doesn't seem like something Red would do, so we'll leave an asterisk by Peacock's name.

Several references were made regarding something that may have happened when Fay accompanied her husband on a trip to Oregon. Red himself mentioned it as a reason to eliminate her.

Then there was Red's missing brother, Gilmore "Gilmer" George Hall. The only record on him that turned up during research for this book was his 1934 marriage license. Samuel testified in court that the family had heard from Gilmore in November 1936, and at that time he was in California, but the elder Hall didn't mention *how* they had heard from him. Most likely by mail, and since Red had sent a Christmas card to Katy Bryant from California in 1944 to cover up Fay's disappearance, it's only natural to wonder if he used the same ruse to hide possible fratricide. He would have been only fifteen years old if he did kill his brother, but we know by a statement from Chief Martin and by Samuel Hall's courtroom testimony that Red was just fourteen when he went to Kansas by himself, so why not to California at fifteen? And there was that strange response he gave when Sheriff Caple asked if he'd had anything to do with his brother's disappearance. "He left home, and I suppose someone murdered him."

How about the six murders investigated by the Texas Rangers? It's highly unlikely that Hall had anything to do with the deaths of Hazel and Nancy Frome in Van Horn, Texas. Torture wasn't his style. The most plausible theory about this crime was that the ladies' Packard had been mistaken for another similar vehicle seen in the area. The second car was used by known dope smugglers who were in debt to a drug ring, and the ring's enforcers mistook the Fromes for the double-crossing mules. That would explain the torture and damage done to the car—a search for answers, drugs or money.

Captain Manuel Gonzaullas mentioned four other murders, but too little is known about the two couples murdered in New Mexico in 1938. Hall was killing migrant farm workers in Arizona that same year, so he could have strayed across the state border and committed more bloodshed there. The victims' names and details of their deaths are lost to posterity.

By any estimation, when Hall confessed to seventeen slayings (and insinuated more), he secured his place in the pantheon of serial killers. That term is usually attributed to the late FBI agent Robert Ressler, but German criminologist Ernst Gennat coined the expression *serienmörder* in 1930 when he was writing about Peter Kurten, the Dusseldorf Monster, whose victims included children. Whatever the origin, serial killer describes a person who has murdered three or more people over a protracted length of time. As members of the Bureau's original Behavioral Science Unit (BSU), Ressler and his colleague John Douglas interviewed dozens of convicted serial killers in order to understand better the pathology that drives them to commit murders repeatedly. These studies produced psychological profiles, so Ressler, Douglas and those who followed in their footsteps came to be known as criminal profilers. But long before the movie *Silence of the Lambs* caught the public's fancy and inspired many young people to become the Clarice Starlings of their generation, a brilliant psychiatrist became a pioneer in the field that didn't exist at his time. He amazed detectives with his insight into the criminal mind. In 1956, New York detectives turned to Dr. James Brussel for help in finding a man who had terrorized the city for sixteen years by planting bombs all around the metropolis. Brussel was a man of infinite curiosity and accepted the challenge. He was already interested in studying the known behavior of people in order to learn who they were. He told the investigators that the Mad Bomber was middle-aged, of Slavic origin, lived in western Connecticut with an older female relative and that when found, he would be wearing a double-breasted suit—buttoned. Late one night, when fifty-three-year-old George Metesky was arrested at the Connecticut home he shared with his two sisters, he asked to be allowed to change out of his pajamas. As he left with the police, he was dressed in a double-breasted suit—buttoned.

Profilers are able to determine personality traits, backgrounds and motives that serial murderers have in common. Some law enforcement professionals scoff at profiling, calling it too generalized to be of any worth, while other investigators, such as those on the Mad Bomber case, welcome profilers and ask them for help in analyzing troublesome cases.

How does Red Hall compare to other serial killers? According to a 2005 study by psychologists Heather Mitchell and Michael G. Aamodt, 36 percent of serial killers were mistreated physically as children and 50 percent suffered psychological abuse. Connie Weir said her cousin Red's childhood was fraught with peril, his father inflicting both mental and physical harm on him. She witnessed the abuse herself.

Another life experience that Hall had in common with others of his ilk was the head injury he sustained as a child. Severe head trauma can factor into the formulation of a serial killer. Damage to the prefrontal lobe may heighten aggression, affect motor functions and alter personalities. Jackie Anthony commented on Red's sideways gait, and Dr. R.E. Rowland testified in court about a neurological disturbance causing Hall's leg hairs to turn gray.

Profilers divide multiple murderers into two groups: organized and disorganized. In the early killings, long before Fay's, Hall seemed to be organized, carefully choosing his victims and staying alert to any unexpected traffic. He dragged the bodies off the side of the road to avoid immediate discovery. However, Fay's murder was hastily planned, and he did nothing to hide her body. That seemed to be where he went off script. That's when he became disorganized. He began to hitch rides with anyone, including a government employee, the FSA agent who picked him up after he had slain E.C. Adams. He was in a life-and-death struggle with J.D. Newcomb Jr. right beside a busy highway in full view of witnesses (Mr. and Mrs. Parks). He didn't anticipate Newcomb putting up a fight or Mr. and Mrs. Parks driving by at that moment, and the roundabout way he got rid of Newcomb's body left detectives scratching their heads in bewilderment. *Devolving*, a term popularized by the television show *Criminal Minds*, accurately describes a stage in the life of a serial killer when he begins to unravel. If this happens, even an organized killer will become erratic. As ASP detective Sims said after the Newcomb slaying, "He's getting sloppy." The murderer slips up. His thinking is muddled. The time between kills is shorter. In Red Hall's case, he began to improvise after he murdered Fay. The slaying of someone he knew personally—perhaps even loved at one point—may have unhinged him to such a degree that he no longer could control his predatory instincts. Did murdering Fay cause him to go on a killing spree that didn't end until his capture?

Some readers may think that by focusing this book on the killer rather than the victims, he is made to appear more like the rest of us, but that's the point. When political theorist Hannah Arendt first used the phrase "the banality of evil," she was referring to Adolf Eichmann, one of the architects of the Final Solution in World War II. It has since become a trite expression but is no less true now than it was then. Like Hall, Jeffrey Dahmer, aka the Milwaukee Cannibal, was everyman and he was nobody. Dahmer once said, "I should have gone to college and gone into real estate and got myself an aquarium; that's what I should have done." Such normalcy is the mask that serial killers don with frightening results. We all have three parts to our personalities: the public self, the private self and the secret self. Some people who knew Hall saw him as likable. His landlady, Mrs. Rose, described him as "a nice, clean boy," and Sheriff Caple thought he was a "pleasant conversationalist." That was his public self, the one he wanted people to see. In private, he was uncaring toward living creatures, be they human or beast. His closest relations saw this side of him, but to others his cold-blooded attitude was camouflaged by his well-favored features, beguiling his intended victims who associated good looks with virtue. His secret self was the one who left dead bodies in his wake. We have no way of knowing exactly how many people he did kill. Even he didn't know. "There are so many, I can't remember," he said.

After his arrest, Red Hall became as infamous in Arkansas as Jonathan Hardin, but his memory would not endure. Very few people today—even residents of Faulkner County—have heard of him. His obscurity was mostly due to bad timing. The bloodiest war in the history of the world was in its last violent throes. Arkansans were more concerned about soldiers slain in far-off lands than one man who was waging a war of sorts against his own countrymen. If he had lived about two decades later, he might have gained as much fame as the Boston Strangler, who ushered in a new age of serial killers in the early 1960s. Television brought news reports of the Strangler into every living room in America and abroad. Viewers who gathered around their TV sets were transfixed by the grainy black-and-white newsreel footage of a sheet-covered body being rolled out of an apartment house to a waiting ambulance, as news anchor Walter Cronkite's voice-over announced that an unknown person—later nicknamed the "Boston Strangler"—had claimed the life of another victim.

Television gave serial killers the kind of publicity formerly enjoyed by politicians, sports figures and movie stars. Thanks to newspapers and telegraphs, however, Jack the Ripper was the first multiple murderer to have his fame spread around the world while his bloodletting was still underway. Though the recorded history of serial murders dates back to ancient times, the modern era began with Jack, or rather Aaron Kosminski, if DNA on Catherine Eddowes's shawl matches Kosminski's. All of the murders attributed to him happened within an area no larger than one quarter of a square mile, but they fell under two separate jurisdictions: the Metropolitan Police and the City Police of London. A lack of cooperation between those arms of the law was a major hindrance to a successful investigation. Had the LRPD and the ASP been at odds with each other, it would have taken more time to catch Red Hall, and he would have taken more lives. Indeed, he might have eluded capture altogether.

Hitchhiking is as dangerous now as it was in Hall's day, for both the driver and the passenger. Just note some of the nicknames given to the murderers: the I-5 Killer, the Santa Rosa Hitchhike Killer, the I-45 Killer, the Freeway Killer (actually three murderers acting independently). In 2004, the FBI noted a possible pattern of slayings along I-40 through Mississippi, Arkansas, Oklahoma and Texas. Blue and red highway lines on roadmaps, the veins and arteries of our nation, our life's blood just under the skin, so vulnerable.

During research for this book, a rumor surfaced that a song was written about Red Hall long ago, but it couldn't be found. If a reader has knowledge of such a composition, please contact the author. Should this book fail to pluck Hall from the dustbin of oblivion, a song might. He would probably like that.

MAJOR AND MINOR
CHARACTERS

L ife dealt various destinies to the people who had been in Red Hall's
orb of influence.

Lieutenant Deubler, who started his career with the LRPD as a
motorcycle officer, rose in the ranks and in 1946 became the assistant to
Detective Chief Martin. This was an anxious time for Martin. He feared that
a grand jury looking into gambling activity in Little Rock was investigating
him, and he believed Deubler was going to testify against him. On New
Year's Day 1947, he ordered his assistant to accompany him on a drive
to Lakewood in North Little Rock, where they got out of the car. Martin
opened the trunk, took out a sawed-off shotgun and fatally shot Deubler
four times before killing himself with his .45 pistol. Their blood, spilling out
onto a canvas of freshly fallen snow, mingled together like a red Rorschach-
inspired painting. As it turned out, Martin was just being paranoid about the
grand jury. He wasn't a target of the inquiry.

In 1967, J. Earl Scroggin retired from the ASP after a total of forty-two
years as a peace officer. Under state law, retirement was mandatory when
employees turned sixty-five. Through the decades, his dedicated service had
been recognized and rewarded with promotions, and he capped his career
as Major Scroggin.

Joe Wirges provided stories for many of the detective magazines of the
era. In the late 1940s and early 1950s, a popular true crime radio program,
The Big Story, featured episodes based on his exploits. He seemed to have a
photographic memory for details about each case he had covered—not just
exact names and dates, but what the weather was like on any particular day,
what kind of gun was used and how many shots were fired. At the end of each

radio show, the sponsor, Pall Mall cigarettes, paid the reporter $500, a nice supplement to Wirges's $60 per week paycheck from the *Gazette*. Upon his retirement, the Pulaski County Sheriff's Office made him an honorary deputy, the ASP made him an honorary captain and the LRPD gave him an engraved detective lieutenant's badge. Joe Wirges died on December 28, 1972.

A few years after working on the Hall case, Alan Templeton was injured in a shootout in Newton County. Two other lawmen had tried to serve commitment papers on a man named Heywood Brown, but he met them with a hail of gunfire. Templeton was among the reinforcements called in to assist. During an attempt to flush Brown out of his house with tear gas, Templeton sustained a bullet wound in the shoulder. The drama ended when Brown set his house on fire and then shot himself to death. Templeton is also mentioned in a book called *The Disappearance of Maud Crawford* by Beth Brickell. Formerly an actress, Arkansas native Brickell became an award-winning writer, producer and director. She has researched and written extensively about one of Arkansas's most intriguing cases, the 1957 vanishing of Camden lawyer Maud Crawford. Alan Templeton was by then captain of the ASP Criminal Investigation Division, and Odis Henley was the ASP's lead detective on the Crawford case. Henley found evidence implicating Henry Myar "Mike" Berg, a member of the Arkansas State Police Commission. Henley passed all his notes on up the chain of command to Templeton. The next time he looked in the file, his notes had disappeared as mysteriously as Maud Crawford herself.

Jake Sims, the little guy with a formidable reputation, stayed on as the unorthodox police chief of Seminole, Oklahoma, for twenty years. In 1952, he became director of the Oklahoma State Bureau of Investigation, serving there for four years. After that, he opened his own detective agency in Oklahoma City. Upon retirement, he returned to Seminole and remained there until his death in 1966.

Dallas chief of detectives J.W. Fritz was on duty when President John F. Kennedy was assassinated in 1963. He was among the men who interrogated Lee Harvey Oswald and was present when Jack Ruby killed Oswald. Fritz testified at the Warren Committee meetings.

Della Fogerty lived to the age of ninety-five, indicating once again that the people from Enola and surrounding communities have often been blessed with long lives. During an interview, she talked about Red's head injury. "Yes, yes, and that's something we may never know. The old saying is, 'Don't try to put the puzzle together until you get all the pieces.' We may never have all the pieces."

After divorcing Red, Walcie married again. She died on June 22, 2000, at the age of eighty-five. Red and Walcie's son served in the U.S. Air Force, married and had children; three weeks shy of his thirtieth birthday, he died, cause unknown.

BIBLIOGRAPHY

Ancestry.com. U.S. Headstone Applications for Military Veterans, 1925–1963.

Anthony, Jackie. Interviews with author. 2011–2012.

Arkansas Democrat. "Ex-Ranger Dies at Age of 75." January 26, 1978.

———. "52 Called to Testify in Hall Case." May 8, 1945.

———. "Hall Admits He Murdered 11 in Arizona, Texas." March 27, 1945.

———. "Hall Willingly Helps Police in Adams Murder." March 27, 1945.

———. "James W. Hall Murder Trial Jury Selected." May 7, 1945.

———. "Last Original State Ranger Is Retired." July 2, 1967.

———. "Officers Seek Identity of Man Brutally Slain." February 4, 1945.

———. "Officers Seek More Data on Hall's Crimes." March 24, 1945.

———. "Police to Take Hall to Scene of Last Crime." March 19, 1945.

———. "Score or More Murders May Be Pinned on Hall." March 23, 1945.

———. "Skeleton Found Where Hall Says He Killed Wife." March 18, 1945.

———. "Slayer Gives Hint of New Developments." March 22, 1945.

———. "Slayer Hall Loses Last Hope of Life." January 3, 1946.

———. "Taxicab Driver Admits Slaying Wife." March 17, 1945.

Arkansas Democrat-Gazette. "All but Two Death Masks of Villains Gone, Forgotten." July 27, 2008.

Arkansas Gazette. "Arkansas's Home-Made Chair Has Killed 168 in 50 Years." September 6, 1963.

————. "Attorney for Hall Appointed." March 29, 1945.

————. "Body Believed to Be that of J.D. Newcomb." March 11, 1945.

————. "Brutal Killer Turns to Bible for Salvation." March 19, 1945.

————. "Calmly Says He Committed Six Murders." March 17, 1945.

————. "Caple Takes Over; Moves Hall to Farm." March 28, 1945.

————. "Cap'n Lee's Pride Is Quiet." January 11, 1953.

————. "Charred Body Found in Car." March 10, 1945.

————. "Driver Found Slain Near Stuttgart." February 11, 1945.

————. "Find Hatchet Thought to Have Killed Kansan." February 9, 1945.

————. "Find Skeleton Proving Hall's Admission True." March 18, 1945.

————. "German Prisoners Glad War Is Over." May 9, 1945.

————. "Hall Accused of Murder of His Wife." March 27, 1945.

————. "Hall Appears Depressed at Being Alone." March 19, 1945.

————. "Hall Executed." January 4, 1946.

————. "'Hall Had Devil in Him,' Father of Victim Says." March 18, 1945.

————. "Hall Placed in Death Cell at Tucker." May 15, 1945.

————. "Hall Reenacts One of Killings for Officials." March 20, 1945.

————. "Hall Resigned to Die; Jokes at Final Meal." January 3, 1946.

————. "Hall Retraces Long Ride with Victim's Body." March 21, 1945.

————. "Hall Sent to Hospital for Sanity Test." March 30, 1945.

————. "Hall Spends Quiet Day on Eve of Trial." May 7, 1945.

————. "He Found Hall 'Remorseless,' Says Dr. Kolb." May 9, 1945.

————. "Jury Declares James W. Hall Slew His Wife." May 11, 1945.

————. "Nazis March Home from Denmark." May 9, 1945.

————. "Negro Murdered and Robbed on Highway." January 18, 1945.

————. "Sheriff Asks Aid of Bus Passengers." March 13, 1945.

————. "Slain Worker Found in Deserted Car." February 4, 1945.

————. "State's Electric Chair Made 50 Years Ago by Professor." April 21, 1963.

————. "Victim Identified as J.D. Newcomb." March 12, 1945.

Blake, Alison. "Blood Bath of the Smiling Slayer." *Inside Detective*, July 1945.

Brickell, Beth. *The Disappearance of Maud Crawford*. N.p.: Luminous Films, 2014.

Chandler, Jim. Interview with author, 2015.

Cook, Bill. Interview with author, May 2016.

Cozy Inn Hamburgers. "The Cozy Inn Story." cozyburger.com/history.

Dayton Beach Morning Journal. August 21, 1948.

El Dorado Daily News. "Laney Will Hear Plea for Hall by Relatives Today." January 2, 1946.

Ellis, Kevin. *The Gaston Gazette*. Interview with author. 2016.

Emporia Gazette. Untitled article about the Lambert/Nipper slayings. November 3, 1944.

Encyclopedia of Arkansas. "Pulaski County Courthouse." https://encyclopediaofarkansas.net.

Faust, Kate. "Remembrances of the Prisoner of War Camp in West Helena, Arkansas." *Phillips County Historical Quarterly*, September 1978.

Find a Grave, findagrave.com.

Fitzhugh, Kathryn. UALR William H. Bowen School of Law, Criminal 4393. Trial transcript: *State of Arkansas v. James Waybern Hall*, #46048. May 1945.

Flame, Antoine. "The Man Who Liked to Kill: Death Rides the Highways." *Detective World*, November 1945.

Fogerty, Della. Interview by the author, July 2013.

Gerrard, R.J. "The Five-Time Killer of Little Rock." *True Detective*, July 1958.

Hope, Charles R., Sr. "Kansas in the 1930s." *Kansas Historical Quarterly*, Spring 1970.

Howard, E. Marshall. "The Kill-Crazy Murderer of Little Rock." *Master Detective*, November 1973.

Iola Daily News. "Conduct Hunt for Slayer of Dr. M. Lambert." November 3, 1944.

Joplin Globe. "Arkansan Says He Killed Nearly 24." March 24, 1945.

Kirksville (MO) Daily Express. "Editorial." November 3, 1944.

Lawton Constitution. "Thugs Hopped When Little Jake Sims Hollered Frog." July 7, 1966.

Lindsey, Michael. *Big Hat Law: Arkansas and Its State Police, 1935–2000*. Little Rock: Butler Center for Arkansas Studies, 2008.

Log Cabin Democrat. "Clemency Is Sought for J.W. Hall." January 3, 1946.

———. "Faulkner Man Put to Death as Murderer." January 4, 1946.

———. "'Haw Haw' Is Put to Death as Traitor." January 3, 1946.

———. "Heavy Fogs Cost 5 Lives in Arkansas." January 4, 1946.

"Lord Halifax, British Ambassador to the United States, visits the U of A." *Arkansas Magazine*, Fall 2015.

Miami Daily News-Record. April 26, 1947.

———. "The Murder of Wehman J. Peacock." October 17, 1944.

Miller, Circuit Criminal Judge L.D. "Murderously Yours." *Vital Detective Cases*, September 1945.

Niagara Falls Gazette. "Taxi Driver Discharged from Navy for 'Indifference,' Confesses He Killed Six Persons, Police Report." March 19, 1945.

"Officers Killed in the Line of Duty." In *History of the Little Rock Police Department*, 17, 18. Paducah, KY: Turner Publishing, 2009.

Oklahoman. "Arkansas Slayer to be Quizzed in City Man's Death." March 19, 1945.

———. "Hall Relatives Seek Arkansas Execution Stay." January 3, 1946.

———. "Slaying Victim Is Identified as W.J. Peacock." October 18, 1944.

Prowling Owl. "Wide Open Kickbacks Are Part of Oklahoma's History." prowlingowl.com.

Pryor Center for Oral and Visual History. Arkansas Memories Project. Ernest Dumas interview. June 4, 2009.

Seminole Producer. "Body of Murder Victim Is Found Among Yule Gifts." December 25, 1940.

———. "Fingerprint Expert to Aid Death Quiz." December 26, 1940.

———. "Killer Search Is Continued." December 29, 1940.

———. "New Suspect in Murder Is Shadowed." December 27, 1940.

———. "Nothing New in Murder Cases." January 24 or 27, 1941.

———. "Two Questioned in Murder of County Oilman." December 25, 1940.

Shea, William L., and Edwin Pelz. *Arkansas Historical Quarterly* 44, no. 1 (Spring 1985): 42–55.

Spade, H.L. "Little Rock's Latest Police Challenge: 'Catch That Hitchhiking Multiple Killer!'" *Official Detective*, July 1945.

Stinnett, Ray. "Crazy to Kill." *Human Detective*, October 1945.

Stories Behind the Big Story. "The Big Story Revealed." sites.google.com/view/thestoriesbehindthebigstory/home.

Weir, Carnella Hall. *Happy Valley Memories: Growing Up on the Farm*. Self-published, 1993.

———. Interview with the author. March 26, 2013.

Wichita Daily Beacon. "Editorial." November 3, 1944.

Wikipedia. "Lord Haw-Haw." en.wikipedia.org/wiki/Lord_Haw-Haw.

———. "Mexican Repatriation." https://en.wikipedia.org/wiki/Mexican_Repatriation#cite_note-:0-1.

Wirges, Joe. *Big Story Radio Show, The.* "Jig Saw." January 26, 1949.

ABOUT THE AUTHOR

J anie Nesbitt Jones began her journalism career by writing features for the *River Valley & Ozark Edition* of the *Arkansas Democrat-Gazette*. After finding her niche as a true crime writer for *AY Magazine*, she acted as a consultant for Investigation Discovery. With her husband, Wyatt Jones, she coauthored two books: *Hiking Arkansas* and *Arkansas Curiosities*. An Arkansas native, she lives in Conway with Wyatt, their two dogs and two cats.

Visit us at
www.historypress.com